浙江省普通高校"十三五"新形态教材 绍兴市重点教材

浙江越秀外国语学院双语示范课程教材

U0647618

Public Relations

公共关系学

李先国 ◎主 编

李映雪 ◎副主编

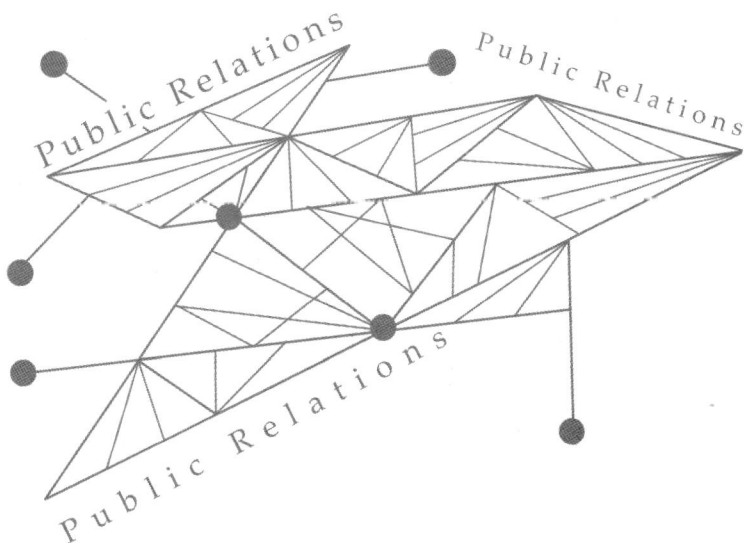

ZHEJIANG UNIVERSITY PRESS

浙江大学出版社

图书在版编目(CIP)数据

公共关系学:英文 / 李先国主编. —杭州:浙江
大学出版社,2021.11
ISBN 978-7-308-21489-6

Ⅰ.①公… Ⅱ.①李… Ⅲ.①公共关系学—高等学校
—教材—英文 Ⅳ.①C912.3

中国版本图书馆 CIP 数据核字(2021)第115034号

公共关系学

李先国 主编 李映雪 副主编

责任编辑	郑成业
责任校对	李 晨
封面设计	春天书装
插图设计	丁杨影
出版发行	浙江大学出版社
	（杭州市天目山路148号 邮政编码310007）
	（网址:http://www.zjupress.com）
排 版	杭州朝曦图文设计有限公司
印 刷	杭州钱江彩色印务有限公司
开 本	787mm×1092mm 1/16
印 张	11.25
字 数	311千
版 印 次	2021年11月第1版 2021年11月第1次印刷
书 号	ISBN 978-7-308-21489-6
定 价	39.00元

Preface

About the Author

Ph. D. Lee Singher, a professor working at School of Network Communication, Zhejiang Yuexiu University, is a judge expert of Shaoxing Time-honored Brand Association.

He has published more than 40 papers, 4 monographs, 1 thesis collection and 1 textbook. Many articles were forwarded and reprinted. In 2014, he won a scholarship for overseas students funded by the Chinese government. He has completed two general projects in Zhejiang Province, is leading one key project in Zhejiang Province, and has participated in two national social science fund projects. He has won four awards above the municipal level, such as the Scientific Research Achievement Award of Colleges and Universities in Zhejiang Province. Since 2014, he has been mainly engaged in teaching and research of public relations, audio-visual language, American drama appreciation and criticism, advertising appreciation and copywriting, and new media writing. He has undertaken 8 times the teaching of "Public Relations" as a bilingual demonstration course at the university, and presided over the compilation of the corresponding textbook as a "Key Textbook in Shaoxing" and a "New Textbook in the 13th Five-Year-Plan of Zhejiang Province".

At present, the main research directions of Professor Lee are public relations and cultural studies.

Building Your Abilities through This Book

Public relations is emerging as a major force in a growing global information society with social media in the 21st century. Beginning in the early 20th century, public relations as a discipline is still relatively young, but it's been on the way to mature, emerging with a management-oriented, relationship-building focus among its stakeholders with more and more emphasis on media tools and behavioral change. For those planning for public relations careers, this book provides a foundation for them. The book also meets the needs of those planning for other professional and managerial careers that require an understanding of public relations concepts and management practices.

This book will be taught by using multi-medium, stressing basic concepts and basic theories, paying more attention to help the students master the basic skills, applying public relations theories into company strategies in order to strengthen the ability to combine theories with practice, master the structure and contents of textbook, deepen the comprehension and application of basic knowledge so as to enhance the interest of their study.

Upon satisfactory completion of the book, students should:

Be able to understand the concepts and principles of public relations;

Enhance their ability to analyze and solve problems;

Familiarize themselves with the approaches, techniques and policies of public relations;

Apply a series of basic public relations principles to practice;

Integrate with other subjects and combine relative business skills and principles together in order to gain a comprehensive perspective on business world.

Course Description

Public Relations is a basic course for Journalism and Communication major and related majors such as Management. This course introduces students the basic concepts, theories, and areas of study that comprise the field of public relations, aiming at helping the students lay a solid fundation of research and work in the field of public relations in the future. This course will enable the students to understand and master the basic concepts and theories, strengthen their ability to engage in the theoretical research and practical work, to think independently, and to analyze and solve the problems. Throughout this course we will discuss the impact public relations has on society and economic development.

In the course of Public Relations you will learn about the theory and practice of public relations, how public relations operates in organizations, its impact on the public and its functions in society. You will study the professional development of the field; concepts, issues, and principles in the practice; and models and theories guiding the practice.

Public relations mainly studies the information communication and communication relationship between social organizations and the relevant public. It is an applied communication science in which social organizations can shape a good image and strive for public understanding and support under the conditions of modern commodity economy, democratic politics and information society. It is also an art of operation and management in which modern organizations seek unity and development.

The main contents of this book include "9Ps":

Professional Introduction to Public Relations;

Periods in the History of Public Relations;

Participation of Public Relations in Management;

Practitioners and Organization—the Subject of Public Relations;

Public—the Object of Public Relations;

Planning of Public Relations;

Publicity—the Naivety of Public Relations Communication;

Practice of Public Relations Special Activities;

Promotion of Organization Image with Public Relations.

Public Relations is an emerging discipline which focuses on the research of the communication behaviors, laws and methods between organizations and the public. It is a comprehensive, applied and new discipline which emerges from the cross-discipline integration of modern communication, management and social psychology.

Every chapter includes at least three extended cases embedded in the main text illustrating how real companies, organizations, and people have addressed public relations challenges. Cases in this book include "4Rs":

Replay of the Event, we will briefly describe when and where someone did something and the main information of the event;

Response, we will narrate the response of the main parties involved in the incident;

Result, we will describe the incident and what the response of the parties ultimately produced, and how it ended;

Reflection, we will analyze the experience and lessons of this incident and the response of the parties from the perspective of public relations principles.

Each of them draws on original, real-world events or incidents in recent years to provide students with a strategic approach to meeting the needs of a client before, during, and beyond a campaign. Using these cases, students explore successful contemporary campaigns and evaluate best practices in all major areas of public relations activity. This practical, client-oriented text shows students how to systematically evaluate and adapt to the needs of a particular client—whether big or small, global or local, for-profit or nonprofit—in order to launch the most effective campaign. Each case includes a brief introduction focused on fundamentals and core competencies, and all cases have been carefully selected to present a wide range of client types in the public relations field.

CONTENTS

Chapter 5 Public—the Object of Public Relations / 77

Chapter 6 Public Relations Planning / 91

Chapter 1
Professional Introduction to Public Relations

Preparation for **S**tart

You have worked hard but it was a tough year for you working in marketing, or you have spent two years studying advertising. In the challenging experience you have learned how to be more self-motivated. You have learned that understanding how customers think is the most important part of your job, so you feel you are more prepared now to be in any other work such as management. Public relations also has a management function.

Understanding **O**bjectives

After studying Chapter 1, you should be able to:

1. Define public relations as the management function that emphasizes building and maintaining relationships between organizations and their publics.

2. Distinguish between the public relations and marketing functions of organizations, identifying the exchange between provider and customer as the distinguishing characteristic of marketing relationships.

3. Define and differentiate among related concepts, including interpersonal relations, advertising, marketing, pulling relationship, and news communication.

Basic **C**oncepts and **E**lements

The thought of public relations originated from the rulers' understanding of public power. After the rulers realized the public power, they wanted to improve their images in the public. In practice, the rulers realized that improving their images should be based on communication, which gradually formed a new discipline—public relations.

Public relations is emerging as a major force in a growing global information society in the 21st century. Beginning in the early 20th century, public relations as a discipline is still relatively young, and it did not really explode until after World War II. Since its beginning, public relations, the new independent modern science, has attracted people's attention and gradually become the objective practice in modern society.

Public relations is the theoretical summary of public relations practice activities, which deepens people's understanding of public relations and plays a guiding role in the healthy development of public relations activities. Public relations activities are rich and colorful, and the understanding of public relations is deepening. The theoretical summary of public relations is constantly sublimated. Therefore, public relations, the new discipline, will have broad prospects for development.

The research object of public relations is the phenomenon and internal law of public relations practice activities. Specifically speaking, the research contents mainly include the theories of public relations, the practice of public relations and the history of public relations.

With the globalization of the world, science and technology, especially information technology, are changing with each passing day. With the increasingly extensive communication and contact among people and the diversity of their means and methods, as well as the continuous and in-depth development of public relations practice, the research objects and subject contents of public relations will become increasingly affluent. This is a burgeoning and vigorous new discipline, and its development prospect will be brilliant.

Definition of Public Relations

In September 1989, Yu Mingyang of Shenzhen University and Liao Weijian of Sun Yat-sen University debated whether the essence of public relations is "image building" or "communication management" at the second National Joint Conference of Provincial and Municipal Public Relations Organizations, which started the debate on the core concept and basic category of public relations. Ming Anxiang and Xiong Yuanwei are the representatives of "image theory". Ju Yan'an and Ji Huaqiang support the "communication theory". The third popular view at that time was "relationship theory", which said that public relations was "relationship coordination" between organizations and the public. The debate lasted until the mid-1990s. In November 1994, *Public Relations Daily* launched a "discussion on the core concepts of public relations". Liao Weijian and Yu Mingyang reiterated their "communication theory" and "image theory" in the discussion. Shen Zhiping of Shanghai Urban Construction University proposed "participation theory", while Li Daoping of Anhui People's Publishing House advocated "coordination theory". On the basis of introducing the development of foreign public relations theories, Guo Huimin proposed that we should not be "paranoid about one theory", but should consider the key words of communication, understanding, image, relationship and development.[1]

What kind of discipline does public relations belong to? It should be identified by its research object, research task, specific research content, guiding ideology of the discipline and basic methods used in the research. Because its content involves the diversity of categories in terms of the discipline system construction and development, it comprehensively uses the principles of many basic disciplines and applied disciplines as well as some of the latest achievements, so there are considerable differences in the judgment and recognition of its disciplinary attributes. At present, there are mainly five popular views.

First, communication theory. This view emphasizes that public relations is a kind of communication activity, which follows the law of communication. Therefore, public relations science should belong to the category of communication science.

For example, the American scholar Fraser P. Seitel believes that public relations is a planned process to influence public opinion, through sound character and proper performance, based on mutually satisfactory two-way communication.[2]

Second, organizational behavior theory. This view holds that the main body of public relations is social organizations. Social organizations carrying out public relations activities, in essence, is a kind of social organizational behavior, which must be based on its specific principles and norms. Therefore, public relations belongs to the discipline category of organizational behavior.

The definition of public relations in the *Great Dictionary of Chinese Occupation* compiled and printed by the Ministry of Labor and Social Security of China is: a practical activity engaged in the investigation, consultation, planning and implementation of public information dissemination, relationship coordination and image management of organizations.

Third, sociology theory. This view emphasizes that public relations is a kind of social relations, and the study of public relations should be carried out within the framework of social relations and according to sociological theories. Therefore, public relations belongs to the category of sociology. At present, the National Classification Guide of Philosophy and Social Sciences regards public relations as a secondary discipline of sociology. Yale professor and *Public Opinion Quarterly* founder Harwood L. Childs concluded that the

---

[1] HU B J. Theory Construction and Intellectual Heritage of China's Public Relations in Recent 30 Years[EB/OL]. [2021-2-20]. http://cjjc.ruc.edu.cn/fileup/HTML_EN/20140202.shtml.

[2] SEITEL F P. The Practice of Public Relations[M]. Twelfth Edition. Beijing: Tsinghua University Press, 2017: 5.

essence of public relations "is not the presentation of a point of view, not the art of tempering mental attitudes, nor the development of cordial and profitable relations". Instead, he said, the basic function "is to reconcile or adjust in the public interest those aspects of our personal and corporate behavior which have a social significance"[①].

Fourth, management theory. This view holds that public relations has management functions, and public relations is applicable to management theories and knowledge. Therefore, public relations belongs to the category of management science.

American scholar Dr. Rex F. Harrow believes that public relations is a unique management function. He collected almost 500 definitions and then identified major common elements in an attempt to define public relations—

Public relations is the distinctive management function which: helps establish and maintain mutual lines of communication, understanding, acceptance and cooperation between an organization and its publics; involves the management of problems or issues; helps management keep informed about and responsive to public opinion; defines and emphasizes the responsibility of management to serve the public interest; helps management keep abreast of and effectively utilize change, serving as an early warning system to help anticipate trends; and uses research and sound and ethical communication as its principal tools.[②]

American scholars Cutlip and Center believe that public relations is a kind of management function to determine, establish and maintain the mutual beneficial relationships between an organization and all kinds of public who decide its success or failure—

Public relations is the management function that establishes and maintains mutually beneficial relationships between an organization and the public on whom its success or failure depends.[③]

Fifth, comprehensive discipline theory. This view holds that each branch of discipline has its own emphasis and emphasizes one aspect of public relations respectively, which is reasonable to some extent, but none of them can reflect the whole picture of public relations. Therefore, public relations is a new, modern, marginal and interdisciplinary subject.

For example, there is a theory of communication management: Professor James Grunig of Maryland University, an academic authority of contemporary American public relations, believes that "public relations is the communication management between an organization

---

① CHILD H L. An Introduction to Public Opinion[M]. New York: John Wiley and Sons, 1940: 3, 13.
② HARLOW R F. Building a Public Relations Definition[J]. Public Relations Review 2, 1976(4): 36.
③ BROOM G M. Public Relations[M]. Beijing: China Renmin University Press, 2013: 7.

and its public"①.

To establish a broad, realistic, and accurate description of the public relations function—four scholars from four universities in the U.S. offer the following working definition:

Public relations is a leadership and management function that helps achieve organizational objectives, define philosophy, and facilitate organizational change. Public relations practitioners communicate with all relevant internal and external publics to develop positive relationships and to create consistency between organizational goals and societal expectations. Public relations practitioners develop, execute, and evaluate organizational programs that promote the exchange of influence and understanding among an organization's constituent parts and publics.②

We agree with the fifth view. Public relations is an independent comprehensive social science, which belongs to an applied discipline. Public relations has four comprehensive characteristics: first, it is both comprehensive and marginal; second, it is both theoretical and practical; third, it is both extensive and open; fourth, it is both technical and functional.

To sum up, public relations refers to the relationship between an organization and the public. The state of public relations is the objective relationship and public opinion between an organization and its public environment. First of all, public relations exists objectively. Secondly, there is a close relationship between the state of public relations and the activities of public relations. Public relations is the communication management between an organization and its related public, whose purpose is to establish a relationship of mutual trust with the public.

The Elements of Public Relations

The practical activities of public relations are a series of public relations work, which use the method of communication to coordinate the social relations of the organization, influence the public opinion about the organization, shape the good image of the organization, and optimize the operating environment of the organization. The practical activities of public relations are a part of organization and management activities and a special function of organization and management.

---

① GRUNIG J E, HUNT T. Managing Public Relations [M]. New York: Holt, Rinehart and Winston, 1984: 6.
② LATTIMORE D, BASKIN O, HEIMAN S T, et al. Public Relations: The Profession and Practice[M]. 4th Edition. New York: McGraw-Hill, 2012: 4.

In a word, public relations includes five basic elements:

(1) The main body of public relations is organization;

(2) The communication object of public relations is the relevant public;

(3) The working means of public relations is the media of communication;

(4) The process of public relations is the two-way exchange of information;

(5) The goal of public relations is to establish a good public image for the organization.

The word "image" borrowed by public relations is not limited to the category of individual, specific and intuitive, but also has a deeper meaning:

(1) The essence of the image of public relations is reputation, and the essence of paying attention to the image of organization is to attach importance to the reputation of organization (the core of public relations image of an organization is the public's cognition and evaluation of its credit);

(2) Public relations puts the connotation of building and improving the image of the organization in the first place, and then considers the appearance of the image of the organization (the overall characteristics and actual performance of the organization are the origin of the image, and the reality of the image is the first);

(3) Public relations shapes the overall image of the organization, not limited to the individual, specific product image or personnel image elements;

(4) The public relations image is to influence the concept and attitude of the public through communication activities.

Public Relations Discipline: From Public Relations Activities to Public Relations Concepts

The state of public relations is not only the basis of public relations activities, but also the result of public relations activities.

An important sign of public relations activities' consciousness and scientificity is that there are modern and scientific public relations theories as guidance.

The concept of public relations is a kind of management concept and philosophy that influences and restricts the policies and behaviors of organizations. It not only guides the healthy development of public relations practice, but also penetrates into all aspects of managers' daily behavior, and becomes a kind of value concept and behavior criterion guiding and regulating organizational behavior.

The image concept of public relations shows that the subjects attach great importance to their own reputation and image in decision-making and other actions; the public concept of public relations shows that leaders and managers attach great importance to the interests of the public; the communication concept of public relations shows that operators and managers have strong communication consciousness and desire; and the coordination concept of public relations is beneficial for adjustment, balance and unification. The concept of mutual benefit in public relations shows that equality and the pursuit of win-win result are regarded as the code of conduct for dealing with various relations in communication and cooperation; the service concept of public relations is shown as a spirit of dedication to others and society.

Dissemination and communication are the process and mode of public relations activities. The communication of public relations activities have various forms, including interpersonal communication, organizational communication, public communication and mass communication. Also it could be sorted as verbal communication, written communication and non-verbal communication.

In short, organization is the main body of public relations activities, namely, the undertaker, implementer and actor of public relations. The public is the object of public relations communication. Public relations, as a discipline, studies the public mainly from the perspective of communication objects, including the general characteristics of the public and the specific characteristics of each target public, the psychological and cultural factors affecting public behavior and public opinion, different types of public relations and their corresponding policies and activities, and the role and significance of some major public relations for organizations.

The Difference and Connection between Public Relations and Related Concepts

▶ Interpersonal Relations

The main differences between public relations and interpersonal relations are as follows:

(1) The main body is different. The subject of public relations is the organization, which deals with the relationship between the organization and the public, while the subject of interpersonal relation is the individual, dealing with the relationship between individuals.

(2) The service objects are different. Public relations serves the organization; the harmony or conflict of relationship will benefit or damage the organization. While interpersonal relation serves the individuals; the good or bad relationship will benefit or damage the individuals.

(3) The scope of communication is different. Public relations should often organize special activities, with the help of the news media to expand the influence and communication scope, while the scope of interpersonal communication is much smaller and simpler.

However, public relations and interpersonal relations are closely related. First of all, public relations is usually expressed as interpersonal relations. Because the relationship between organizations as a whole is often expressed through the connection between several people in one organization and a number of people in another organization, which is also a kind of interpersonal relationship. Therefore, public relations is often carried out by means of interpersonal communication. For example, the relationship between stores and consumers is generally manifested as the relationship between salesmen and consumers. Secondly, to achieve the goal of public relations, the coordination of interpersonal relations is indispensable. Since the relationship between the organization and the public is generally reflected through interpersonal relations, only by coordinating the interpersonal relations inside and outside the organization can good public relations effect be produced.

▶Advertising

Advertising is a kind of paid communication, that is, advertisers pay to buy the right to use the media to promote their products, services or ideas. In public relations activities, advertisements are often used to expand the influence. However, there are some differences between public relations and advertising, specifically as follows:

1. Different Goals

The goal of advertising is to sell more products and services in the shortest time with the least cost. The goal of public relations is to establish the image of the whole organization, to enhance the understanding of the people inside and outside the organization, so as to make the cause of the whole organization successful.

2. Different Ways of Communication

The information dissemination of advertisement is to transform the information of products or services into written manuscripts, design them into patterns, and use sophisticated techniques to make advertising films and TV clips. The basic principle of advertising is to attract people's attention. The information dissemination of public relations is the same as that of news covers, that is, speaking by facts, there must be no falsehood, and "truthfulness and credibility" is its basic principle. The key to the success of public relations personnel lies not in the use of literary and artistic means of communication, sensationalism and deliberate description, but in the selection of appropriate opportunities, the adoption of appropriate forms, and the timely and accurate transmission of news-worthy information to the specific public through appropriate media.

3. Different Communication Cycle

Generally speaking, the communication cycle of advertising is short. Usually, a certain product or service is publicized in a certain period. It has obvious seasonality and periodicity. In contrast, the communication cycle of public relations is long-term, because the goal of public relations is to establish the image and credibility of the organization. This is not a temporary effort. It requires prolonged, planned and step-by-step work.

4. Different Nature of Work

Advertising is a kind of local work in enterprise management. The success or failure of an advertisement generally does not have a decisive impact on the overall operation of the enterprise. However, public relations work is in a global position in business management and is a kind of strategic work. The quality of public relations determines the image and reputation of the organization, and thus determines the survival of the organization.

5. Different Effect

The effect of advertising is direct and measurable. The benefit of an advertisement can be measured by the increase of sales volume and profit. The effect of public relations is quite different from that of advertising. Successful public relations makes an organization have a good reputation, which benefits the organization immensely. However, it is difficult to measure the benefits by simple hard indicators.

Public relations and advertising have the above differences, but they are also closely related, which is mainly manifested in the following aspects: public relations needs to use advertising forms as a tool, and advertising business also needs the guidance of public relations ideas. For the sake of the overall situation, it is often necessary to make advertisements carry out public relations work, that is, the so-called "public relations advertising". However, this kind of advertisement is not to promote the specific products or services of the enterprise, but mainly introduces the management, personnel quality, service purpose, obligations and responsibilities for the society, good deeds and so on. Its purpose is to create a good image of the enterprise. General commercial advertisements need to be guided by public relations and incorporated into the overall strategy of public relations. The effectiveness and achievements of a company's public relations work may fall short because of an exaggerated advertisement.

►Marketing

Marketing is a kind of business activity in the trading area characterized by equivalent exchange, in which industrial and commercial organizations publicize products to customers by various means, so as to stimulate their purchasing desire and behavior and increase the sales volume. As a means of sales promotion, public relations is being paid more and more attention and used by the industrial and commercial circles. However, there are also important differences between public relations and marketing: public relations pursues the social and long-term interests of the organization, while marketing pursues the economic benefits and short-term interests of the organization. Actions to improve the social benefits of an organization and consider its long-term interests are undoubtedly conducive to improving the economic benefits and short-term interests of the organization, though sometimes there are contradictions.

Generally speaking, marketing techniques have a clear flavor of promoting products, which makes consumers feel that there is a selfish purpose of industrial and commercial enterprises behind them. Therefore, whether it is prize sales or installment payment, consumers will instinctively generate resistance psychology, which greatly reduces the effectiveness of these marketing techniques. Over time, consumers will even be disgusted with these marketing methods, thinking that they are selling overstocked goods and refuse to buy them. Therefore, the combination of public relations practice and marketing activities can solve this problem to a certain extent. Public relations practice focuses on communicating feelings with consumers, so that consumers can have a correct and comprehensive understanding of enterprises and their commodities, and on this basis, establish the image or trademarks of the enterprises. With the progress of public relations work, salesmen can get good results when they're selling goods in a friendly and trusting environment.

▶"Pulling Relationship"

"Pulling relationship" refers to the improper interpersonal activities such as "setting up personal relationship", "finding a way out" and "going through the back door". On the surface, the direct purpose of public relations and "pulling relationship" seems to be the same. They both hope that through interpersonal communication, the organization or enterprise can get the support of relevant parties, so as to solve problems smoothly. Therefore, some people think that as long as this goal can be achieved, any means can be adopted. But in essence, the purpose and function of public relations is to fight against the bad phenomenon of "pulling relationship". Therefore, there are essential differences between the two.

First, they have different social bases. Public relations is a product of the rapid development of commodity economy, the rapid expansion of information dissemination and the unprecedented complexity of modern economic life. "Pulling relationship" is a product of the closed and backward feudal economy. It came into being under the condition of low level of social productivity and insufficient goods and services.

Under the condition of highly developed commodity economy, enterprises encounter competitors, the traditional seller's market is gradually transformed into the buyer's market, and consumers have a choice. It is important for enterprises to survive and develop. How to expand the influence of enterprises in the public has become a significant issue for modern entrepreneurs. Due to the expansion of information dissemination, enterprises need to timely and effectively transmit their own information to the public in the vast ocean of information, and also to timely and fully feed back the external information. Due to the unprecedented complexity of modern economic life, enterprises are facing a series of new problems. All these problems need to be deeply studied and taken seriously, and a group of professionals who are familiar with public opinions and information dissemination are needed to solve them. Public relations is a summary of such practical experience.

Second, they have different purposes. The pursuit of public relations is that the economic benefits of enterprises are basically consistent with the interests of the public. Through long-term, planned and effective public relations work, the enterprise will establish a good image in the society, and the enterprise will continue to develop under the premise of being consistent with the public interest. The basic stance of "pulling relationship" is to benefit oneself at the expense of others, and to seek the private interests of individuals or small groups. Social interaction is regarded as a privilege to seek personal interests, and various social relations are regarded as private property and vested interests of individuals or small groups. As a result, individuals tend to fill their own pockets, while the social and public interests are seriously damaged.

Third, they use different means. Public relations is mainly based on the principle of information dissemination to transmit all kinds of necessary information to all walks of life in a timely and effective manner. At the same time, it provides decision-makers with the social public's response and forecast of social environment and its changes, establishes a two-way information circulation network, and improves the scientificity and efficiency of economic management. The main means of public relations are various: newspapers, radio, network, magazines, internal publications, news documentaries, television films, etc. And "pulling relationship" secretly uses improper ways and means, even by means of violating the law and discipline, in order to meet the private interests of individuals or small groups. Its means are nothing more than eating, drinking, pulling, boasting and clapping. It is forbidden in terms of public relations professional ethics.

▶News Communication

There are two kinds of news communication: propaganda and news release. Propaganda is a kind of one-way psychological induction, behavior influence and public opinion control; news release has the dual functions of reporting and publicity. The main difference between public relations and news communication lies in the differences between their tasks and the objects they must be responsible to. In order to understand the organization's public relations activities, it is necessary to adopt a public relations approach. News communication must be responsible to the whole society.

In order to survive in the society for a long time, an organization can not only consider the immediate interests, but also obtain social understanding and support by creating social benefits. This is why organizations need public relations practice. Therefore, the starting point of public relations work is to safeguard the long-term interests of the organization. However, in order to achieve this goal, the practitioners have to be responsible to the society, open the truth to the public and let the public know about the organization. Although the starting point is different, public relations and news communication still have a very similar position in specific actions, that is, they must speak on the basis of facts.

Through the mass media, news can be quickly spread out in the society, producing a wide range of influence. Public relations work often functions with the help of this characteristic of news. Therefore, writing press releases and establishing good relations with the press have become one of the daily tasks of public relations staff.

Public relations news should also abide by the principles of news reporting, and should not boast. That is to say, it must have authenticity, timeliness and novelty or freshness.

Another remarkable phenomenon is the use of "news making" method in public relations activities. For an enterprise, if it wants to get more consumer support, it must improve its popularity and reputation. If the enterprise can often play a leading role in news reports, it is undoubtedly very beneficial to achieve this goal. Therefore, public relations personnel should strive to make the enterprise the focus of news reports without any fraud. For this reason, public relations personnel often have to aim at the interests of the public and the press, plan and take the initiative to "create" some news, so as to attract the attention of the press and the public.

Compared with general news reports, the method of "news making" has the following characteristics:

First, it is planned and arranged by public relations specialists on their own initiative, not by accident, and thus more in line with the needs of the organization.

Second, because of the "making", that is, "manufacturing", or the processing of events, this kind of news is often more dramatic, more able to cater to the public interest and attract the public's attention.

Third, on the basis of the above two points, the effect of "news making" is often prominent. As the focus of news reports, organizations often become the center of people's temporary conversation, thus enhancing the organization's visibility.

Learning to Practice

Scan to Read More

After graduating from a private college in Shaoxing, your cousin went home to inherit his father's business and took over the towel factory that his father had run for many years. He found that the profits of the towel factory increased year by year, but the external publicity was not enough. He decided to establish a public relations department. He thinks that the public relations department can create more featured stories and newsletters to tell the the history and philosophy of the factory. He heard that an excellent reporter was just laid off the post, and he wanted to hire him. But after knowing that your school has a public relations major, he wants to hire a public relations graduate. In a dilemma, he asked you to give some advice. What advice would you give him concerning the recruit?

Indication for Answer

It would be better to hire someone with a degree in public relations because they can not only do publicity and have a variety of other technical skills, but also they have been educated to assist the organization in adapting to its publics. It would not be better to hire someone with an master's degree in business administration though public relations is a management function. Because public relations involves more than just publicity and other technical skills, it requires information that those with master's degree in business administration don't have as indicated by many specialties. While it's true that the first public relations practitioners were former reporters, public relations has evolved to include so much more than "telling our story" that hiring a reporter is an inadequate rationale.

You cannot ignore the reality that publicity still plays an important role in many public relations programs; while it is true that the practitioners cannot control publicity, lack of control hardly makes publicity "dangerous".

In addition to publicity, the practitioners should also have communicating and technical skills, as well as management skills such as planning, monitoring, analyzing, counseling, etc. It attempts to inform the executive director of the full range of public relations activities. Someone may state that publicity is the primary tactic used in public relations, typically negating the need for other approaches to solving public relations problems. Yes, it is. But this option simply perpetuates the myth that publicity alone can solve most public relations problems. Likewise, reinforcing the executive director's perception of public relations as publicity would be a disservice to your cousin, to whoever takes the position, and to the field of public relations.

Case Study   PUBLIC **C** RELATIONS

Case 1.1   Zhong Nanshan Thanked JD

▶Replay of the Event

On the evening of January 31, 2020, JD Logistics customer service received a phone call from Zhong Nanshan's academician team of Guangzhou Respiratory Health Research Institute, the First Affiliated Hospital of Guangzhou Medical University. Then, JD Logistics responded as soon as possible, coordinated the railway transportation capacity, and transported the batch of materials to Wuhan at the fastest speed. On the morning of February 2, JD Logistics delivered 100 oxygen generators to Hankou Hospital with its own transport vehicle and handed them to the hospital staff. Zhong Nanshan wrote down his thanks to JD Logistics: "Thanks to JD's heart attached to the front line of medical aid, delivering urgently needed medical materials to Wuhan as soon as possible."

As of February 6, JD Logistics has delivered more than 2.36 million pieces of medical and epidemic prevention materials from more than 30 cities across the country, including masks, medical gloves, goggles, disinfectants, etc., through the deployment of road, railway, aviation and other resources to major hospitals in Wuhan, Huanggang and other places.

During the epidemic in 2020, JD did not directly give money, but donated materials. However, JD Logistics opened a special channel to help Wuhan and other places, so that materials can be delivered quickly. JD's logistics performance is really awesome and fast, which has aroused netizens' praise. JD also seized Zhong Nanshan, a powerful person who can attract the attention of netizens. Zhong Nanshan has become the mainstay of people's hearts in this epidemic. He is an individual full of positive energy. Everything he has done and every word he said has convinced netizens.

►Response

JD Health CEO Xin Lijun joined the renowned respiratory scientist Zhong Nanshan, epidemiologist Li Lanjuan, WHO Representative in China Dr. Gauden Galea, and other medical experts from China, ROK, and Japan to share their epidemic fighting experience with the world during a webinar entitled "COVID-19 International Experience Sharing and Exchange".

To ensure medical supply, JD has leveraged its supply chain advantage to make sure at least 2 million disposable medical masks are available for daily sale via its first-party stores. This is an increase of 600% compared with that in February. Other kinds of masks, such as KN95 and KF94, can be purchased whenever consumers need on JD.com.[1]

►Result

JD has done a good job in public relations. Responding quickly to and cooperating actively with Zhong Nanshan helps to get JD a high and positive evaluation. In the marketing of major e-commerce giants, JD also performs well.[2]

►Reflection

Public relations shapes the overall image of an organization, not limited to the individual, specific product image or personnel image elements.

The concept of public relations is about management philosophy that influences and restricts the policies and behaviors of organizations. It not only guides the healthy development of public relations practice, but also penetrates into all aspects of managers' daily behavior, and becomes a kind of value concept and code of conduct of the organization.

---

[1] ZHANG H. JD Joins Chinese Medical Experts Sharing Anti-Virus Experiences[EB/OL]. [2021-2-26] https://jdcorporateblog.com/jd-joins-chinese-medical-experts-sharing-anti-virus-experiences/.

[2] https://www.sohu.com/a/372245587_663169.

Case 1.2 Chairman of Home Original Chicken Tears Employee Joint Letter

▶ Replay of the Event

Home Original Chicken is the largest fast-food chain in Anhui Province, with more than 800 stores in the country. In the middle of China's COVID-19 outbreak, Home Original Chicken Chairman Shu Congxuan posted a video speech revealing billions in losses and the closing of over 100 franchises. "I am even willing to sell assets like real estate and cars. I'll try my best to maintain the jobs of my 16,328 employees." Shu Congxuan, founder and Chairman of the Chinese fast-food chain, told the audiences in the video, which named as "Chairman Shu Congxuan Tearing Employee Joint Letter", and triggered a screen swipe. In the video, Shu Congxuan personally appeared on the camera to tell us that due to the impact of the epidemic, the Home Original Chicken was damaged by 500 million yuan, and he was grateful to the employees in Wuhan for delivering meals to the medical staff. He advocated that all people should be quarantined at home and contribute to the country. In addition, more activities should be carried out at home. In the end, Shu Congxuan tore up the no-salary letter from employees, which was said to be full of positive energy.

▶ Result

After the video was sent out, it quickly went viral and was highly praised. The voice of "China's good boss" was constantly heard, and the local chicken also properly absorbed a wave of fans.

▶ Reflection

This is a very successful public relations marketing event. Whether it's deliberate marketing or revealing the truth, it's been highly effective.

Case 1.3 Ali Invests in Tea

▶ Replay of the Event

On August 27, 2019, Weibo account Tianyancha revealed that Suzhou Yuanchu Investment Partnership (Co., Ltd.), the company invested by Alibaba, took a stake in the online black milk tea store, Chayanyuese, which is based and merely operated in Changsha.

Before that, the boss of Chayanyuese had claimed that he had no money and would not open a branch in other cities. Many "small owners"—customers who wanted to drink but could not drink it looked at "tea" and sighed. Netizens speculated that Chayanyuese would finally have the money to go out of Hunan and open branches across the country.

►Response

On August 27, Chayanyuese's official Weibo account released "Some Explanations about the Scandal with 'Father Ma'", saying that "Alibaba shares" is not accurate, but only Ali's indirect investment; Chayanyuese has been looking forward to expanding the market outside of Hunan Province, but has no specific time and plan. "Maybe it's going slower, but I'd like to go steadily."

►Result

This response is undoubtedly a pot of cold water for tea fans in other places. However, after the response, the positive emotions of netizens increased instead.

►Reflection

The credits for the increase should go to the copywriting of Chayanyuese's statement which was praised by netizens: "Chayanyuese's copywriting has always been very comfortable, giving people the feeling that they are very sincere"; "I hope that all the artists' publicity teams can learn from Chayanyuese and see how others declare this style of writing."

Courseware   Quiz

Chapter 2
Periods in the History of Public Relations

Preparation for Start

Scan to Dialogue   Scan to Listen

In your previous job, you took charge of new employee training. You thought you didn't like public speaking, but you have learned communicating and leading skills by interacting with many people. Your friend values the importance of reliability and leadership at work. He feels obligated to accomplish his duties well. Because he once took charge of new project implementation, in which he led five team members as the team leader. He became more comfortable dealing with work and people thereafter. Both of you have leadership experience. The work of many people forms part of the history of public relations.

Understanding Objectives

After studying Chapter 2, you should be able to:

1. Trace the evolution of public relations from the germination to its American modern practice.

2. Name major historical leaders in public relations and describe their respective contributions to the development of public relations and current practice.

3. List five performances in the development of public relations in contemporary China.

Basic Concepts and Elements

The Germination of Ancient Public Relations

As a discipline, public relations originated in the United States, but the idea of public relations has sprouted in ancient times.

Throughout the history, as early as ancient Egypt, Babylon, Persia, ancient Greece, ancient Rome, rulers used force and public opinion as tools to control the society and handle the relationship with the people. These emperors and governments spent a lot of money and manpower building up statues, temples, mausoleums as well as writing hymns. They used exquisite artistic techniques to describe their heroic achievements, establish their prestige, publicize their great and sacred identities, and spread the knowledge they believed. They have a strong sense of public relations.

In ancient Greece, there were people who lived by writing hymns. Aristotle, a famous ancient Greek scholar, made a brilliant exposition on how to use language to influence the thought and behavior of the audience in his book *Rhetoric*. The book is known as the first monograph on public relations theory. The ruler of ancient Rome, Caesar founded and published the world's earliest daily newspaper, *Diary*. He also wrote a documentary book recording his achievements, *The Battle of Gaul*. This book was once called the first-class public relations book by some famous Western experts. The successful spread of Ancient Christianity in the world is also regarded as another model of ancient public relations.

The Development of Public Relations in the United States

▶ Public Relations before the Founding of the United States

It can be said that American public relations originated from the struggle of the North American colonial people who fought against autocracy and strived for independence.

The leaders of the time were good public relations propagandists. They used newspapers, pamphlets, flyers, events, meetings and debates to promote their independence. One of the representatives is Samuel Adams. Some of his theories and practices are still valuable for today's public relations. Adams believed that all people are much more governed by feelings than by reason. Therefore, he believed that public opinion comes from the progress of things and the way in which the public observes the progress of things (not only depending on the objective things themselves). Adams was an aggressive public relations expert with a set of successful technologies. He created some events to obtain the support of the public, and then achieved his own goals.

These events played an important role in organizing the anti-British struggle in 13 colonies of North America.

These technologies are as follows:

(1) An organization may complete an action through a public relations activity, such as the "Sons of Liberty" organized in Boston in 1766 and the "Committees of Correspondence" established in Boston in 1775.

(2) The use of emblems, such as "Liberty Tree" to enhance public recognition, makes it easy to identify and induce the public emotion.

(3) The use of slogans can turn a complex problem into an easy one and repeatedly enhance the public cognition. The slogan "Taxation without representation is tyranny" is such an example.

(4) The use of events can attract public attention and trigger discussion, thus promoting the formation of a clear public opinion, such as the Boston Tea Club incident.

(5) Make one's own point of view consistent with the public in an event, so that the interpretation of the event can be accepted by the public, such as the Boston Massacre.

(6) In order to carry out public relations activities as much as possible, we must use public relations technology and various communication channels to infiltrate new ideas and views into the public. In the 34 years from 1750 to 1783, Adams and others published more than 1,500 pamphlets attacking British rule, many of which were written by Adams himself. Adams also painstakingly established the communication committee of 13 colonies to inform the British rulers of their misdeeds and maintain regular contact with the 13 states.

Alexander Hamilton's main contribution was leading a campaign for the ratification of the constitution. From October 1787 to April 1788, at the critical moment of how to establish the United States, Hamilton published a series of remarkable and far-reaching articles, which skillfully guided the public opinion at that time and promoted the realization of the federal system in the United States. Historians consider the event as the best public relations work in history.

The first government public relations and campaign think tank emerged in the days of Andrew Jackson. Amos Kendall was the main representative of public relations activities in this period. In the late 1920s and early 1930s, ordinary citizens began to have the right to vote. The political interest of the public germinated rapidly, and the role of the press was increasingly obvious. Jackson was a military hero and head of state who valued intellectuals. He hired scholars and journalists to set up a brain trust to advise him. Kendall was a journalist in the think tank. He was Jackson's campaign agent and public affairs expert. He was responsible for arranging interviews with reporters, writing and releasing speeches to the press, conducting opinion polls and news analysis. He founded the earliest organ of the U.S. government, *The Globe,* as a mouthpiece to report and explain the government policy, and gradually developed a set of White House publicity methods.

During this period, there were several things closely related to public relations. In 1842, Harris Berg's newspaper *Pennsylvania* and Rory's newspaper *Star* printed some public opinion votes and sent them to readers to predict the outcome of the presidential election. These were the first public relations surveys. The emergence of news agents in 1860 was the beginning of the combination of news and industry. In 1882, Eaton of the United States delivered a speech on public relations and legal responsibility at Yale Law School, which is regarded as the earliest speech concerning public relations.

The public first recognized public relations in 1899. In that year, George Westinghouse, the inventor of alternating current, firstly organized a special public relations department in the modern sense. He employed E.H. Heinriches, a journalist from Pittsburgh, as his news consultant, and successfully made alternating current accepted by the society.

▶The Development of American Modern Public Relations

The development of American modern public relations has experienced the following periods:

1. Barnum Period: Myth and Deception

Public relations in this period is also known as one-way boasting public relations, which is the prelude of professional public relations represented by press propaganda activities.

In the first half of the 19th century, with the advancement of political democratization and the improvement of public status, the cause of mass communication developed rapidly. It was at this time that press propaganda activities became popular where some companies or enterprises employed special personnel to carry out propaganda in newspapers and periodicals for their own interests. In the 1830s, *The New York Times* took the lead in launching a "penny movement", that is, a newspaper could be bought for a penny. With its low price and content of concern for the public, the newspaper has been recognized and accepted by the whole society, and has made the government departments and various magnates compete for it as an important tool to influence the public opinion. However, due to the large circulation and high operating cost, the advertising expenses also soared. For that reason, some big companies had to hire some reporters or propagandists to fabricate news about themselves and their organizations and even myths to attract readers' attention.

The most representative newspaper propagandist in this period was Phineas Taylor Barnum, who, the owner of a circus, is famous for making and fabricating myths. His living time witnessed an important evolution in public relations, and its influence still exists today.

Barnum's most typical propaganda was the myth that a black slave in his circus, named Hayes, raised George Washington, the first president of the United States. After the story was published, it caused a sensation. Barnum took the opportunity to send letters from readers to newspapers under various pseudonyms, which caused a controversy. As a result, many people went to the circus with curiosity, which made the box office revenue increase dramatically. After Hayes died, the autopsy showed that she was only 80 years old, not 160 years old as Barnum advocated, and it was impossible for her to raise President Washington.

But Barnum claimed that he was also the victim. As a matter of fact, Barnum has already benefited a lot from the controversy he orchestrated.

Barnum's creed is that the public should be fooled and all propaganda is good. His behavior of boasting, deceiving and creating myths for himself or his organization by any means, regardless of public interests and professional ethics, is totally contrary to the purpose of modern public relations, and is a disgraceful page in the history of public relations.

2. Ivy Lee's Period: Professionalization of Modern Public Relations

The public relations in this period was one-way communication.

This period saw the beginning of professional public relations with the main idea that organizations must be frank and open to the public. Ivy Lee was a representative of this period.

In the end of the 19th century, the United States has entered the era of monopoly capitalism. A small number of enterprise oligarchs hold almost half of the economic lifeline of the country. They extracted surplus value by unscrupulous means and implemented a closed and confidential policy in operation, which was known as the "ivory tower". Their cruel exploitation caused strong dissatisfaction among workers, increasingly tense labor relations, intensified class contradictions, sharp interest conflicts among various classes and groups, and the public was full of hostility to the enterprise oligarchs. In this case, a news movement with the theme of exposing industrial and commercial enterprise scandals broke out, which was known as "muckraking journalism" in history.

Henry Demarest Lloyd, a journalist working for the *Chicago Tribune*, published a series of articles exposing corruption in business and politics in the early 1880s. These articles included "The Story of a Great Monopoly" (1881) and "The Political Economy of Seventy-Three Million Dollars" (1882) in the *Atlantic Monthly*, "Making Bread Dear" (1883) and "Lords of Industry" (1884) in the *North American Review*, which caused a stir and Lloyd has been described as America's first investigative journalist.

Ida Wells was another journalist who attempted to use her writing skills to stimulate social change. In 1884 she began teaching in Memphis. She also wrote articles on civil rights for local newspapers and when she criticized the Memphis Board of Education for under-funding African-American schools, she lost her job as a teacher. Ida used her savings to become a part owner of *Free Speech*, a small newspaper in the city. Over the next few years she concentrated on writing about individual cases where black people had suffered at the hands of white racists. This included an investigation into lynching and discovered during a short period 728 black men and women had been lynched by white mobs. Of these deaths, two-thirds were for small offences such as public drunkenness and shoplifting.

On March 9, 1892, three African American businessmen were lynched in Memphis.

When Ida wrote an article condemning the lynchers, a white mob destroyed her printing press. They declared that they intended to lynch Ida but fortunately she was visiting Philadelphia at the time. Unable to return to Memphis, Ida was recruited by the progressive newspaper, *New York Age*. She continued her campaign against lynching and Jim Crow laws and from 1893 to 1894 she made lecture tours in Britain. In 1901 Ida published her book, *Lynching and the Excuse for It*. In the book she argued that the main aim of lynching was to intimidate the blacks from becoming involved in politics and therefore maintaining white power in the South.[1]

Investigative journalism became a movement in 1902 when magazines such as *McClure's Magazine* and *Everybody's Magazine* joined who in the struggle for social reform. These magazines became extremely popular and other mainstream publications such as *Cosmopolitan* and *The Saturday Evening Post* began publishing articles exposing corruption in politics and business.

President Theodore Roosevelt responded by initiating legislation that would help tackle some of the problems illustrated by these journalists. This included persuading the Congress to pass reforms such as the Pure Food and Drugs Act (1906) and the Meat Inspection Act (1906).[2]

Samuel McClure established *McClure's Magazine*, an American literary and political magazine, in June 1893. Selling at a low price of 15 cents, this illustrated magazine published the work of leading popular writers such as Rudyard Kipling, Robert Louis Stevenson and Arthur Conan Doyle.

In 1902 the magazine began to specialize in what became known as "muckraking journalism". On the advice of Norman Hapgood, McClure recruited Lincoln Steffens as editor of the magazine.

Lincoln Steffens recruited Ida Tarbell as a staff writer. Tarbell's articles on John D. Rockefeller and how he had achieved a monopoly in refining, transporting and marketing oil appeared in the magazine between November, 1902 and October, 1904. These materials were eventually published as a book, *History of the Standard Oil Company* (1904).[3]

A group of young and honest journalists bravely acted as "ugliness fighters". Their sharp views pointed to those illegal tycoons and corruption of the government, exposing their ugly deeds in broad daylight. In 10 years, more than 2,000 articles of this kind have

---

[1] https://spartacus-educational.com/Jmuckraking.htm.

[2] https://spartacus-educational.com/Jinvestigative.htm.

[3] https://spartacus-educational.com/USAmcclureM.htm.

been published in various newspapers and magazines. Some even set up magazines to expose ugliness, which has made many big enterprises and capitalists infamous. At first, the monopoly consortia tried to calm down the public with high pressure. First, they tried intimidation, then threatened not to put advertisements in magazines that exposed ugliness, or used bribes as "weapons", or continued to create "myths" and cover up scandals by running their own newspapers and periodicals. As a result, contrary to their wishes, public hostility to monopoly oligarchs kept growing. The "muckraking journalism" and the strike movement at that time brought a fierce blow to those monopoly oligarchs.

Under the attack of "muckraking journalism" and strike movement, American economic circles began to face up to the important influence of the press and the public on the development of enterprises. They began to change their thinking mode in order to get rid of the crisis.

DuPont was one of the first to wake up.

DuPont Company, in full E. I. duPont de Nemours & Company, was an American corporation engaged primarily in biotechnology and the manufacture of chemicals and pharmaceuticals. The company was founded by Éleuthère Irénée duPont (1771-1834) in Delaware in 1802 to produce black powder and later other explosives, which remained the company's main products until the 20th century, when it began to make many other chemicals as well.[1]

At that time, since the technology was not very mature, some explosion accidents were inevitable. At first, the company adopted a confidentiality policy, and thus all reporters were not allowed to take interviews. As time went by, the company has left a terrible image of "bleeding killing" in the public mind, which had a very negative impact on its marketing share and enterprise development. DuPont asked his friends in the press for advice. They suggested that he implement the "open door" policy and turn the "ivory tower" into a "glass house". DuPont accepted the proposal and invited one of his friends to be the director of the company's information department. Later the company changed its past practice and insisted on disclosing the company's information to the public. At the same time, it carefully designed a slogan: "Chemical industry can make your life better!" In addition, it actively sponsored public welfare undertakings and organized voluntary services on the streets, which altered the company's bad image gradually.

As a result, many companies started to hire news spokesmen to carry out public relations measures such as factory opening, visit and introduction, and used mass media to

---

[1] https://www.britannica.com/topic/DuPont-Company.

build their own "glass house".

In the upsurge of creating a new image for enterprises, a new profession was born, and Ivy Lee was the pioneer. Ivy Lee graduated from Princeton University and was a journalist for *The New York Times* and *The New York World*. He believed that simply exposing the dark side is a negative approach and by this means, only half of the problem could be solved. The best way to eliminate misunderstanding is to tell the truth to the media and adopt a policy of information disclosure, which can both promote the development of the society and supervise the enterprise behavior. In order to realize his ideal, he set up Parker and Lee Company with George Parker in 1903, and became the first professional public relations practitioner to earn commission by providing services for customers. Ivy Lee's public relations thought was that "the public must be told quickly"—to "tell the truth" to the public. That is why we call the industry at this time "one-way information dissemination".

Ivy Lee also dealt with the crisis for Rockefeller Foundation and Pennsylvania Railway Company, as well as reshaped the images of these consortia or companies. From then on, he has become a famous public relations expert and was reputed as "the father of public relations". In 1903, Ivy Lee opened the first publicity consulting firm (in fact, the first public relations company) and became the first professional public relations person to charge fees for providing services to clients. In 1906, the famous landmark declaration of principles was issued. Its creed was "the public must be informed", and the "open door" and "tell the truth" priciples were put forward.

3. Edward Bernays' Period: Public Relations Is a Science

Public relations in this period was known as two-way communication, when it became a science from an art.

The dominant idea of this period was "to be liked by the public", and its representative person was Edward Bernays, a great master in the history of public relations. In 1923, he first taught Public Relations course at New York University. In the same year, he published the "first milestone" monograph *Crystallizing Public Opinion*, which expounded the concept of "public relations counsel". *Public Opinion* was written in 1928 and *Public Relations* was published in 1952. Bernays' main contribution is separating the theory of public relations from the field of journalism and communication, which eventually became an independent and completely new discipline.

After Ivy Lee's and Bernay's periods, the public relations in the United States rose rapidly, mainly in the following aspects:

(1) The business community began to gradually promote the public relations system. Bell Company, Ford Motor Company, General Motors Company, Baltimore Railway Company,

Edison Electric Power Company, John and Lawson Iron and Steel Company in the United States all established their public relations departments or hired someone to take charge of public relations work from 1908 to 1913. By 1937, 20% of the largest companies in the United States had established public relations departments.

(2) Public relations consulting industry obtained rapid development. When Parker and Lee was founded, there were only three similar companies in the United States. By 1937, there were about 250 public relations companies and more than 5,000 public relations practitioners in the United States. In 1939, the American Public Relations Council (ACPR) was established under the chairmanship of Dr. Harrow, a famous public relations scholar. In addition, the government's public relations affairs further developed.

(3) Public relations research and education began. Edward Bernays has made outstanding contributions in this period. After graduating from Cornell University in 1912, he began to work in journalism. In 1913, he was employed as the manager of Public Relations Department of Ford Motor Company. During the World War I, Bernays joined the Public Information Committee organized by President Wilson and headed by George Greel. The Committee has raised its ability to report and mobilize public opinion to an unprecedented height. After the war, Bernays and his wife set up a public relations company and began to provide comprehensive PR consulting services for the society. In 1923, he published his first monograph on public relations, *Crystallizing Public Opinion*. In the book, the meaning of "public relations counsel" was clearly discussed, and the principles, procedures and professional ethics of PR work were put forward. This book is known as a milestone in the development history of public relations theories. He developed public relations into a more knowledgable, conscious and organized discipline. He particularly stressed that in public relations activities, we should first understand the public's requirements, and then carry out planned and organized publicity on the basis of determining public values and attitudes. Publicity should be "put to the public's good". This was a great step forward to the one-way communication in the Ivy Lee era.

After Bernays taught Public Relations firstly at New York University, Dr. Harrow opened a Public Relations course at Stanford University in 1937. In 1947, Boston University established the first School of Public Relations.

4. Cutlip and Center's Period: The Humanization of Contemporary Public Relations

The two-way symmetrical public relations is an advanced stage in the development of contemporary public relations, which emphasizes "two-way communication, two-way balance and public participation". The representative figures of this period are Scott Cutlip and Allen Center.

In 1952, Cutlip and Center published an authoritative monograph on public relations—*Effective Public Relations*. The book discussed the "two-way symmetrical" mode of communication. As the goal of PR work, the interests of the organization and the public should be placed in the same important position; as a method, the two-way communication between the organization and the public is indispensable. This book has been reprinted many times since its publication and is known as "the Bible of public relations".

There are two theoretical premises for the two-way symmetrical model: One is to regard public relations as a closed system or an open system; the other is to regard public relations as functionary or functional.

To regard public relations as a closed and functionary system is to put the PR personnel in the position of communication technology implementers, who make regular press releases to maintain and promote the public's good impression of the organization, while neglecting to collect feedback information from the environment.

To regard public relations as an open and functional system is to establish the maintenance and change of the relationship between the organization and the public on the basis of the interaction of output-feedback-adjustment. The public will be absorbed into the dominant coalition of decision-making. Public relations can not only play the role of adviser and consultant in decision-making, but also a warning role which helps prevent potential crisis.

The mode of two-way symmetrical communication embodies the "win-win" philosophy advocated in modern competition, that is, both sides can achieve common development.

The Development of Public Relations in China

China is an ancient civilization. The thoughts and activities of "public relations" can be traced back to ancient times with written records. The "public relations" activities of the rulers came into being in the Shang Dynasty, and the tribal leaders have realized the importance of utilizing public opinion. In Pan Geng's story of moving the capital, he put forward in three speeches that "I am very respectful to accept the people's orders", which proves that he has learned how to obey the public opinion and win the people's trust. Only by explaining reasons of moving the capital to the people could his intention be realized.

In ancient China, the technology of collecting and utilizing public opinion also witnessed great progress. In order to control the flood, Yu the Great once "met the princes at Tushan". After consultation, he finally got the support of all the people, and then he was able to command thousands of troops to complete the feat of flood control. In the Zhou Dynasty, the court had a system of "collecting poems", one of the purposes of which was to observe the people's feelings and public opinion. "Zi Chan does not destroy the Township School" in *The Chronicle of Zuo* reflected the supervision on public opinion and the two-way communication between intellectuals and political power. Shang Yang of the Qin Dynasty used the "man-made event" of "reward for moving wood" to win the trust of the people, which showed his determination to reform and set up a reliable image among the people. In ancient China, the techniques of persuasion and communication have been quite developed, and have become an important means to create public opinion and coordinate various social relations. For example, Su Qin traveled around the country to publicize the theory of "alliance" and maintain the peace for more than ten years, thus becoming a typical case of "three-inches-tongue is better than a million strong soldiers".

Leaders of peasant uprising in the past dynasties also paid great attention to creating public opinion and winning support of the people with various means of communication. From Chen Sheng, Wu Guang to Li Zicheng and Hong Xiuquan, they all had their own classic practices. In some economic activities in ancient China, people consciously or unconsciously used multiple means of communication to publicize themselves and establish their good reputation and images. Zhang Qian's access to the Western regions and Zheng He's voyages to the West occupied a very important position in the history of world public relations.

In 1934, the Journalism Department of Yenching University introduced courses such as "Practical Propaganda and Public Relations" "Public Opinion and Propaganda" from the United States.[1]

In the early 1980s, public relations spread rapidly in China. In 1983, the functional departments of public relations began to appear in domestic enterprises; in 1985, domestic universities began to set up relevant courses or majors; in 1986, public relations associations in various provinces and cities were gradually established; in 1987, the China Public Relations Association was established in Beijing, marking the formal recognition and acceptance of public relations in China; in 1991, the China International Public Relations Association was founded, marking that China's public relations has been in line with international standards.

The development of China's public relations has gone through four stages: the introduction period from the late 1970s to the early 1980s, the high-speed development period from the mid-1980s to the early 1990s, the professional development period from the 1990s to the beginning of the 21st century, and the network and new media era in the current time.

---

[1] WANG X L. The Beginning and End of the Public Relations Education During the Period of the Republican China[J]. Journalism and Communication, 2010(6): 55-60.

Next, we will look over the development of China's contemporary public relations from several aspects, such as practice, communication and education, theory research, and organization construction.

►Introduction and Development of Public Relations Practice in China

In 1980, China set up three special economic zones in Guangdong Province: Shenzhen, Zhuhai and Shantou. Not long after that, some hotels in Shenzhen and Zhuhai set up public relations departments according to some foreign management models, and introduced the functions of public relations. Soon, the public relations department of Beijing Great Wall Hotel successfully planned a PR activity to invite the U.S. President Reagan to hold a thank-you banquet in the hotel. Public relations became famous all over the country overnight, showing its charm to the Chinese people who started to look at public relations with great respect.

In 1984, Guangzhou Baiyunshan Pharmaceutical General Factory took the lead in setting up a public relations department, which was the first public relations department in Chinese mainland.

In 1985, Hill+Knowlton Strategies, one of the largest international public relations companies based in the United States, set up an office in Beijing. In July 1986, China Global Public Relations Company, the earliest professional public relations company in Chinese mainland, was founded. Since then, more and more organizations have realized the importance of public relations and have set up PR departments or hired full-time PR personnel. Over the past 30 odd years, China's public relations cause has created a series of miracles and accumulated a number of classic cases with Chinese characteristics.

With the further development of market economy, not only tourism hotels and enterprises of daily necessity production have introduced public relations, all walks of life have known more and better about PR business. Some cities and regions have also applied public relations in their image strategy, and the government is attaching more importance to the research and use of public relations.

In May 1999, the Ministry of Labor and Social Security officially recognized public relations as a profession.

On January 4, 1999, the Ministry of Labor and Social Security officially approved the establishment of the Public Relations Committee of the National Vocational Qualification Working Committee. The committee has formulated professional standards for public relations, compiled textbooks for professional training and qualification, and launched assessment mechanism for PR personnel.

▶A Large Number of PR Talents in China Have Been Trained through Public Relations Education

In 1985, the Department of Communication of Shenzhen University founded the first Public Relations major in Chinese mainland. In the same year, various public relations classes and lectures were held in Guangdong Province and Beijing. A number of colleges and universities began to set up related courses. In 1994, the State Education Committee approved Sun Yat-sen University to officially set up a four-year undergraduate Public Relations major. At present, China's public relations education has been standardized, systematic and multi-level. There are high-level bachelor's degree, master's degree, doctor's degree and postdoctoral degree in Public Relations. There are also various forms of continuing education and training for public relations talent. Currently, there are more than 1,000 universities offering public relations courses in China, and dozens of colleges and universities offer related programs.

In December 1989, the National Seminar on Public Relations Teaching in Colleges and Universities was held in Shenzhen. At the seminar, the teaching syllabus and teaching plan were put forward after research and discussion. Subsequently, two to five national public relations teaching theory seminars were held in Hangzhou, Lanzhou, Beijing and Wuhan, which played a positive role in promoting public relations education in China. Various levels of discussion and education have trained a large number of PR talents for the country and prepared human resources for the development of China's public relations.

In November 1986, Ming Anxiang and others published the first public relations book in China, *The Art of Image Building: An Introduction to Public Relations.* Since then, Liao Weijian of Sun Yat-sen University, Ju Yan'an of Fudan University, Xiong Yuanwei of Shenzhen University, Ji Huaqiang of Xiamen University and Guo Huimin of International Relations University have successively published teaching materials, some of which have been reprinted several times.

▶ The Theoretical Research Promotes the Development of Public Relations Practice

As early as February 1984, when *Economic Daily* reported the public relations experience of Baiyunshan Pharmaceutical General Factory in Guangzhou, it published an editorial entitled "Research on Socialist Public Relations", which inspired people to study and create public relations theories and practice. Since the establishment of China Public Relations Association in 1987, it has made unremitting efforts.

In 1990, China Public Relations Association held the first National Symposium on Public Relations Theory in Xincheng County, Hebei Province, with the theme of "public relations and social development". In May 1991, China Public Relations Association held a national working conference in Beijing to summarize and exchange experience on the development of public relations. In their congratulatory speeches, experts fully affirmed the achievements made in China's public relations industry, and clearly pointed out the development direction and fundamental tasks of this area. At that time, it was a great impetus to the public relations cause. At the same time, China Public Relations Association, Beijing Public Relations Association, Department of Mass Communication of Shenzhen University, *Public Relations* magazine, *Public Relations Guide*, *Beijing Public Relations Newspaper* and *Public Relations Newspaper* jointly organized the PR work evaluation of China's top ten outstanding enterprises, which set up some successful examples and summed up abundant effective experience.

After the Xincheng conference, China Public Relations Association has organized a national theory seminar every year. Following China's domestic conditions, participant of these conferences have discussed the basic theories, applied theories and frontier science of public relations, which effectively promoted the in-depth study in this field.

For example, in July 1992, the Academic Committee of China Public Relations Association held a seminar on "the characteristics of China's public relations" in Shandong Province. In 1993, it held a seminar on "re-exploring the characteristics of China's public relations" in Huairou District, Beijing, and then launched a textbook, *Chinese Public Relations*.

In 1997, the first Cross-Strait Public Relations Theory and Practice Seminar was held in Taiwan. Scholars and professionals jointly discussed the theoretical and practical issues of public relations, creating a precedent for cross-strait cooperation in public relations.

▶Organizations of Public Relations in China

In November 1986, Shanghai Public Relations Association, the first public relations association in China, was established. In May 1987, China Public Relations Association, a national public relations organization, was established in Beijing. Since then, various provinces, cities and autonomous regions have followed suit. In April 1991, China International Public Relations Association was established, which promoted the internationalization of China's PR industry.

Within the enterprises, the established public relations departments have been gradually exploring the organizational structures suitable for China's domestic conditions on the premise of introducing and learning from the foreign experience. Outside the enterprises, there are a number of public relations agencies. Some enterprises and institutions employ public relations consultants and experts, planning groups or other forms to promote their PR undertakings.

Over the past 30 odd years, public relations in China has developed rapidly and achieved remarkable results in theoretical research, practice, and education. The world has been impressed by the achievements, but there are still some problems throughout the field to be better resolved.

▶The Division of Public Relations Community in China

From the middle and late 1990s, China's public relations community began to differentiate. Due to the lack of financial support from the practical circles, the *Public Relations Guide* and the *Public Relations Journal* stopped publication successively in 1995 and 1997. *Public Relations* magazine was also suspended and transferred to other journals, but only *Public Relations World* magazine managed to survive. Public relations organizations that once sprang up like mushrooms after a spring rain have mostly declined due to lack of funds. Some "only have one brand left"[1] and most of them have disappeared.

The division of the theoretical circle is more obvious. The public relations researchers who were "halfway through the road" in sociology, literature and other fields have returned to their respective majors. Some public relations scholars have become "trendsetters" in the market torrent, making reports, planning and running companies all over the country, with no extra time or energy to attend related meetings. The industry is calling for a strong impetus to revive."[2]

Learning to Practice

Scan to Read More

You are going to class in the morning. When you have breakfast in the canteen, your friends see that you are holding Professor Li's *Public Relations*, talking about the recently popular TV series *Perfect Relationship*, and they exclaim that your professional course is fashionable. Please cite some facts to show that the principles of public relations have been used for a long time and that the unique contributions made by some historical figures still

---

① HU B J. Theory Construction and Intellectual Heritage of China's Public Relations in Recent 30 Years[EB/OL]. [2021-2-20]. http://cjjc.ruc.edu.cn/fileup/HTML_EN/20140202.shtml.

② *Ibid.*

play a guiding role in dealing with the relationships between various organizations and the public today.

Indication for Answer

1. You can start by pointing out that the first use of the term "propaganda" was in the 17th century by the Catholic Church.

2. You then point out that historian Allan Nevins said that Alexander Hamilton, James Madison, and John Jay engineered "the finest public relations job in the history" to gain national acceptance of the U.S. Constitution. This organized effort to urge ratification of the Constitution included the federalist letters written to newspapers.

3. Publicity techniques were even more prevalent at the time of the American Revolution and in all subsequent conflicts or situations when power has been threatened or when public support was needed. Samuel Adams initiated what can be called a public relations campaign. Adams recognized the value of using symbols, like the Liberty Tree, that were easy for identifying and arousing emotions. Adams also used slogans that are still remembered, like "Taxation without representation is tyranny". Adams directed a sustained-saturation public relations campaign with all available media. He staged the Boston Tea Party to influence public opinion. As a leader of the Sons of Liberty, he suggested the formation of the Committees of Correspondence and provided the organizational structure to implement the actions made possible by his public relations campaign.

4. When the first publicity agencies were founded, common practices included keeping clients' names secret and paying newspapers to carry the information. Ivy Lee, one of the early pioneers changed these practices with his "Declaration of Principles".

Case Study

Case 2.1　Xibei's "Crying for Poverty"

▶Replay of the Event

After the outbreak of the COVID-19 epidemic, small and medium-sized enterprises all said that life was hard, but most of the complaints were limited to the communication between friends and industries. However, Jia Guolong, Chairman of Xibei Group, was the first to publicly "cry for poverty". The article "Xibei Jia Guolong: The Epidemic Has Caused More Than 20,000 Employees to be Unemployed and We Can Only Afford Three Months' Salary" went viral on the social media, which attracted great attention from people and reaped a wave of Internet browsing. According to the article, Xibei lost 700 million yuan in a month, and the loan used to pay wages was only enough for three months.

►Response

On the second day after the article was widely read, Xibei immediately publicized its takeout service, and said that it would donate from the business to doctors in Wuhan.

►Result

As the Chinese saying goes, "Crying children have milk to drink", many banks took the initiative to find Xibei and the company obtained 430 million credit in five days to pay wages. The Beijing branch of Shanghai Pudong Development Bank offered to provide financial support for Xibei and on Feb. 7, a total of 120 million yuan has been transferred to the restaurant giant's account. [①]Xibei company turned the corner.

►Reflection

Xibei has done a very good job in public relations. Instead of passively facing the enterprise's dilemma, it is better to take advantage of the social hot spots to win sympathy and attention, which can not only spread the brand, but also solve the current plight. Xibei has successfully transformed from crying for poverty into a model of public relations marketing.

Case 2.2 "Employee Sharing" Became an Emerging Trend amid COVID-19 Epidemic

►Replay of the Event

Hema Fresh Store is a new retail format completely reconstructed by Alibaba for offline supermarkets. It is a supermarket, a restaurant and a vegetable market. Consumers

---

① MAY J, LI L F, PENG P G, et al. China Shores up Businesses while Combating Virus Outbreak[EB/OL]. [2021-3-15]. https://english.jschina.com.cn/PhotoGallery/202002/t20200210_6502232.shtml.

can buy things in the store or place an order through its App. One of the biggest characteristics of Hema is the fast delivery: within 3 km around the store, it takes no more than 30 minutes to deliver the goods to your house. On July 14, 2017, Hema started business. On June 11, it was selected into the "2019 *Forbes* list of China's most innovative enterprises".

During the epidemic since December 2019, Hema has been active in delivering Ziroom meals to hospitals in Wuhan and other areas, which has been highly praised by netizens.

After Xibei's "crying for poverty", Hema immediately took action again. Many staffs of Yunhai Cuisine and Youth Restaurant were employed by Hema. More than 1,000 workers of Xibei, Shu Daxia, Wangxiangyuan and Chayanyuese also joined Hema. After interview, physical examination and training, they could take up their posts.

►Response

According to the domestic media outlet *National Business Daily*, more than 3,000 new employees had joined Hema as of Feb. 19, 2020, while over 4,000 people had signed up for the "Talent Sharing" plan under Suning's logistics arm as of Feb. 21, 2020.

►Result

Several companies including domestic retailer Suning and French supermarket chain Carrefour later followed suit. The American supermarket chain Walmart has also joined in the trend, hiring more than 3,000 temporary workers from other sectors to work at its branches in cities like Beijing, Fuzhou, and Shenzhen.[①]

►Reflection

Hema, born for innovation, embodies the concept of sharing. The "employee sharing" action not only solved the problem of staff shortage, but also took on great social responsibility.

The concept of sharing has been very popular in recent years and a hot topic of the Internet attention. Undoubtedly, taking advantage of this concept would benefit companies to a large extent.

---

① CAI X J. "Employee Sharing" an Emerging Trend Amid COVID-19 Epidemic[EB/OL]. [2021-3-20]. https://www.sixthtone.com/news/1005235/.

Case 2.3　Female Internet Star Enters Captain's Cockpit

▶Replay of the Event

On the evening of November 3, 2019, a blogger revealed on the Internet that a female online celebrity entered the cockpit of a Guilin Airlines flight and drew a circle of friends. Why could the star enter the pilot's cockpit and take pictures in a dignified way? Why didn't the crew stop her? As soon as the incident was exposed, it immediately triggered heated discussion among netizens. People were angry at the complacency of the star and the inaction of the crew members, and that the airline was not aware of it. Guilin Airlines dropped into a deep crisis of public opinion.

▶Response

On November 4, Guilin Airlines issued an official notice on the Internet, saying that it attached great importance to netizens' report of "a passenger entering the cockpit". The pilot involved will be banned from flying activities for good, and other crew members will be further investigated. The company also said it would conduct internal self-examination in accordance with aviation regulations.

▶Result

Compared with the resentful emotions before the official announcement, netizens' positive comments on Guilin Airlines increased significantly. Netizens praised Guilin Airlines' zero-tolerance attitude and gave it firm support.

▶Reflection

With the ever-changing world and emerging challenges, an enterprise or organization may encounter public relations crisis at any time, which requires us to respond flexibly on the basis of theory learning.

Courseware　　　　　　Quiz

Chapter 3
Participation of Public Relations in Management

Preparation for **S**tart

How can you show that you have leadership qualities? For example, Zhang Shan shows his initiative when presenting a strategic roadmap to management, and he has successfully achieved key projects with his leadership. While Lei Mei uses her communication skills to persuade managers to go along a different route. She can convince them after one or two presentation sessions. They show their leadership qualities in their work. People with leadership qualities are strongly needed in the public relations industry.

Understanding **O**bjectives

After studying Chapter 3, you should be able to:

1. Outline the six functions of public relations.

2. Define the specific function of public relations such as collecting information and monitoring the environment, providing consultation and suggestions, participating in decision-making, promoting communication and image of an organization, coordinating relations, balancing interests, and eliminating risks and crisis.

Basic **C**oncepts and **E**lements

The function of public relations refers to its role and responsibility in an organization. In a broad sense, the function of public relations is to mobilize all the forces that can be mobilized, use various means to create a good image of the organization, win a good living environment for the organization, promote development of the organization, and make the organization gain an advantage in the fierce competition.

Collect Information and Monitor the Environment

Public relations should first play the role of collecting information and monitoring the environment, that is, as an organization's early warning system, it should predict the trends and evaluate the effects through various investigation and research methods, so as to help the organization maintain a high sensitivity to the complex and changeable environment and keep a dynamic balance with the social circumstance.

Information collection is a prerequisite for public relations. In the modern society, information has become a recognized huge resource. Public relations is an information-oriented industry. Therefore, whether it is internal or external public relations, any planning should start from collecting information, so as to know the "enemy", know yourself and be invincible in a hundred "battles". The function of information collection requires public relations personnel to have information awareness and be alert to relevant organizations at any time.

The so-called "monitor the environment" refers to observing and predicting the public situation and various social conditions that may affect the realization of organizational goals, so as to make the organization keep a clear mind, a keen sense and give prompt responses to the changes and pressure from the environment, and to ensure that the practitioners can scientifically shape the image of the organization.

▶Sources of Information

The public that restricts and affects the survival and development of an organization includes two aspects: internal public and external public. Therefore, the information needed by public relations includes internal or endogenous information and external or exogenous information.

1. Internal (endogenous) Information

Internal information mainly refers to the information and dynamics from various sectors within the organization. The development of an organization is firstly restricted and influenced by its internal public objects, including the management personnel, technical personnel and all staff of other departments. They are in the front line of the daily operation. Their understanding and evaluation of the strategies, finance, and materials within the organization have important information value.

2. External (exogenous) Information

External information refers to the information and dynamics from the external environment in which an organization is located. The external public objects related to the organization are very extensive and complex. Therefore, a wide range of social information networks should be established. We should not only pay attention to the information of the public objects that is obvious enough to know, but also predict the trends. We should neither neglect the public objects with direct interests nor the ones that have indirect relations. For example, the needs of customers, the views of partners, the intention of investors, the dynamics of competitors, the remarks of government officials, the evaluation of the press, the remarks of opinion leaders, etc. Public relations needs to collect a large number of external public information.

►Contents of Information

As the information center of an organization, the public relations department is not limited to the business information directly related to the organization's core interests, but also the social information of politics, economy, culture, science and technology, military affairs, civil conditions and so on.

1. Information Related to Organization Image

Public relations personnel should first pay attention to all kinds of information related to the image evaluation of the organization. This information involves the public's impression, views, opinions and attitudes towards the policies, products, behaviors and personnel of the organization.

(1) Product image information. Product image is the objective basis of organization image. Only when the product is accepted and welcomed, can the value of enterprise be recognized by the society. The public's opinions and evaluation on products are various, such as quality, performance, function, price, style, packaging, and after-sales service.

(2) Organization image information. The overall image of an organization is usually reflected in the public's evaluation of other elements of the organization. For example, the organization's principles and policies; the system, procedures and efficiency; the management level; the strength of technology, finance and talents; the service quality and standard; and the enterprise culture. Organizations need to adjust and improve themselves according to these evaluation information.

2. Various Social Information in the Environment

Public relations departments need to monitor social changes and trends for organizations, pay attention to the dynamics of politics, economy, culture, science and technology, military, fashion, folk customs and other hot issues, analyze their direct or potential impacts on organizations, make full use of favorable factors in the environment, avoid adverse factors, and keep the changes of organization and dynamics in the social environment balanced.

The information collected by the public relations department is generally macro and directional, which cannot be replaced by information from other functional departments of the organization.

Provide Consultation and Participate in Decision-Making

This is the most valuable function of public relations, so it is also called "consulting industry" and "intellectual industry". The World Public Relations Conference held in Mexico in 1978 emphasized the consulting and decision-making functions of public relations.

▶ The Meaning of Consultation

Public relations consultation is to organize PR personnel to provide opinions and suggestions for the decision-making of various management departments, so as to make the strategy more scientific and systematic, and take into account the interests of the public.

The consultation of public relations is closely related to the collection of information. Access to information is the premise of consultation. Only by providing advice and suggestions for the organization can the collected information give full play to its function and realize its value.

▶ Main Contents of the Consultation

(1) To provide advice on the internal policies, procedures and actions of the organization, give full play to the guiding role of public relations in the organization, participate in decision-making, and formulate the goals in line with the development of the organization.

(2) To provide advice on the organization's public relations strategy, marketing strategy, advertising strategy, CIS strategy and organizational culture strategy, integrate the original departments into a system, and formulate a scientific implementation plan for the reference of decision-makers.

(3) To forecast the changes from the environment around the organization, so that the decision-makers could have several options to adapt to these changes.

▶ Ways to Consult

1. Set up a Consulting Service Department

The consulting service department is the think tank of an organization. Its main task is to provide various suggestions for the organization and guide the scientific decision-making.

For example, Guangdong Foreign Economic and Trade Corporation once consulted Guangzhou People's Paper Mill on the introduction of a set of papermaking equipment. Through careful comparison and analysis of the international market price, the project saved foreign exchange of 1 million US dollars for the factory.

2. Help the Organization Choose the Timing of Decision-Making Programs and Activities

The consulting function of public relations is manifested in the use of PR means to evaluate, select and implement relevant decision-making plans for the leaders. Special attention should be paid to the unity and coordination of the economic and social benefits of the decision-making programs, and the decision-makers should be urged to focus on the social impact of their decision-making behaviors. At the same time, we should mobilize all means of public relations to promote the democracy and scientificity of the decision-making process.

In order to raise the popularity of an organization, it is necessary to take part in and hold various public relations activities, such as press conferences, trade fairs, expositions, and news releases. Public relations personnel can choose the right time, place and way to participate in these activities according to their practical experience. Through the activities, the organization can build up it networks and improve its reputation.

3. Participate in Decision-Making

Public relations personnel should not only put forward general consultation suggestions for the organization, but also participate in decision-making as much as possible by offering sufficient information, which directly affects the decision-making process. This is the optimized form of public relations consultation. Public relations personnel should make great efforts to carry out their work. Before making decisions, they should widely consult the public at home and abroad to obtain comprehensive information for the reference of decision-makers, so that the decision-making scheme has strong social adaptability and flexibility. Public relations personnel should use their work achievements and strategic thinking to attract the attention of the leaders, so as to create more opportunities for themselves to participate in decision-making activities.

Communicate to Promote Image

▶Active Communication Can Guide Public Opinion

The communication function of public relations is mainly reflected in two aspects: One is to organize two-way communication with the public through communicating skills, so that an organization can win the trust and support of the public; the second is to create a good public opinion environment for the organization by holding news events, public relations advertising, special activities and so on.

▶The Process of Guiding Public Opinion

In a sense, without the function of communication, public relations will achieve nothing. There are three steps to guide public opinion:

(1) Create public opinion and inform the public (i. e., explain the relevant policies, behaviors and products of the organization to the public, strive for public understanding, and promote public recognition and acceptance).

(2) Strengthen public opinion and expand influence (i. e., use modern media to strengthen the public's impression on the organization, deepen the public understanding of the organization, and improve the social visibility and reputation of the organization).

(3) Guide public opinion and promote the image of the organization.

Coordinate Relations and Balance Interests

▶The Meaning of Coordination

Coordination in public relations is to achieve the harmonious development of mutual benefits between the organization and the public on the basis of communication. The important role of coordination is maintaining the overall balance of the organization and management system, so that all parts can keep pace with each other, give full play to the overall advantages and ensure the implementation of the plan and the realization of the objectives. The Coordination can be divided into generalized coordination and narrow coordination. Generally speaking, coordination includes not only the internal part, but also the external part, such as coordination activities between the organization and the government, the community and consumers. Narrowly speaking, coordination mainly refers to the part within an organization, such as coordination between the upper and lower levels of staff, and coordination among various departments and units in the same level. The aim of public relations coordination is to seek unity within the organization and harmony outside the organization.

Marx said that everything people struggle for is related to their interests. Public relations is also based on an organization's interests. After an organization enters the market, many relations that used to be regulated by administrative means need to be regulated according to economic laws. As an open system, an organization will face all kinds of demands from the public while pursuing its own interests. In order to create a good internal and external environment and coordinate various relations, the organization public relations must first recognize these interests in the principle of sincerity and reciprocity, and then try to meet these interests in the principle of bidirectional symmetry. When different interests conflict, they should be coordinated and balanced in line with the principle of fairness and equality, without discriminating or ignoring the legitimate requirements.

► Assignment of Coordination

Coordination is not only an end but also a means with dual attributes. It's purpose is to gain the ideal state of a relationship; as a means, it needs the practitioner to work hard to adjust the relationship, so it can reach and keep a good state. There are three areas in which public relations can play the role of coordination.

1. The Interests and Relations between the Leaders and Employees within an Organization

The harmonious relationship between leaders and employees in an organization can directly arouse the enthusiasm, initiative and creativity of employees and leaders' willingness to bear responsibilities. It stimulates all employees to become a unity and cohere together for the same task. Therefore, the public relations department and personnel of an organization should strive to coordinate the relationship between leaders and employees. Specifically speaking, on the one hand, public relations personnel should apply scientific methods to publicize the principles and policies of the organization to the employees, convey the management strategy of the leaders, and make corresponding explanations as much as possible, so that the employees can understand and consciously implement them. On the other hand, public relations personnel should constantly and extensively collect employees' perceptions and opinions, and timely convey this information to the leaders, so as to improve and promote the overall work and ensure a harmonious relation between the leaders and the employees.

2. The Interests and Relations among Various Departments and Links in the Organization

Within an organization, due to their respective tasks, different departments often lack the overall concept and act on their own rules, resulting in some contradictions, which may bring unnecessary troubles and losses to the organization. Although the coordination among departments is mainly done by leaders, public relations departments should also play a part in it. Through communication, practitioners should strengthen the contact and understanding among departments, making them support each other, trust each other, understand each other, and work together to improve the organizational performance and achieve organizational goals.

3. The Interests and Relations between an Organization and the External Public

Any organization, in its development process, will have contradictions and conflicts with the external public for various reasons. Once these phenomena appear, the public relations department and personnel should timely understand the situation, coordinate the relations and properly handle the contradictions and conflicts. Otherwise, the development of the organization will be badly affected.

▶Coordination Methods

1. Feedback and Regulation Method

Feedback and regulation method is to adjust the organization's actions according to the information feedback. In the process of feedback, the public relations personnel should inform the internal and external public of the organization's policies, plans and other information. At the same time, they should timely collect and convey the views of the internal and external public to the decision-making level of the organization, so as to remedy the defects or revise the plan.

2. Self-Examination Method

Sometimes the relations between an organization and the public are not smooth. There may be contradictions between the cadres and the masses, between departments within the organization, or between the organization and the community, the consumers, and all levels of agents in the government. On such occasions, the organization should pay attention to self-discipline, carry out self-examination and self-supervision, and take the initiative to correct problems.

3. Emotion Coordination Method

There is an emotional relationship between the organization and the public. If the two sides have good feelings for each other, everything will be easy to handle; if the feelings are not good, there will be resistance. Therefore, public relations personnel should pay attention to the coordination of emotions and be good at eliminating psychological distance between the public and the organization. For example, Joe Gillard is a famous car salesman in the United States. An important reason for his success is that he has established a special relationship with his customers. He said he would do everything possible to get the best for customers when they brought their cars back for repairs or after-sales services. Mr. Gillard would also send customers who had bought cars from him postcards of different sizes and formats each month. The small postcard tied Gillard's heart with the customers' closely. Considerate service and emotion coordination are good ways to establish a good relationship between the organization and the public.

4. Information Sharing Method

The information sharing method is to promote the information exchange within the organization by establishing and expanding various communication channels and coordination mechanisms, so that the situation of the leaders can be transmitted to the staff, and vice versa. This method can strengthen the contact among departments, too. Sharing information can help all members cooperate with each other, so as to improve the centripetal force and cohesion of the organization. For example, a factory has set up a column of "Daily News" on the bulletin board at the gate of the factory, which will be posted before 8:30 a.m., and it will never be interrupted except for holidays. When the employees go to work every day, they first spend a few minutes reading the daily news, so that they can timely understand the main trends and information of the whole plant, including the latest decisions and opinions from the managers, important personnel changes, the latest development of production and operation, welfare information, cultural and entertainment news, and the approval for employees' suggestions. We all feel that this bulletin board is more useful than holding a meeting. Because of theirs love and trust, workers and managers actively provide materials for the editorial department, which greatly strengthens the internal communication and horizontal contact of the organization, straightens out the interpersonal relationship, and effectively gathers all the staff together. With the development of the Internet, they have moved the practice to the factory's website. In the new media era, they put the "Daily News" sector into their official accounts on Weibo, Wechat and Douyin. This information sharing method keeps internal relations harmonious. It can be seen that the higher the degree they share information, the more harmonious the relation is.

5. Negotiation Method

The negotiation method is to avoid or reduce contradictions and conflicts between the organization and the employees or the outside public, so as to keep the loss as minimum as possible.

Cultivate Public Relations Consciousness and the Market

▶ Public Relations Consciousness and Its Main Contents

The public relations consciousness is our rational understanding and general opinion on the essential attributes, characteristics, functions, activity rules and methods of public relations. After the basic needs of life have been met, consumers have gradually developed their consuming level to an economic and cultural one. In corporate public relations, an organization takes consumers as the main public, which plays a cultural construction or shaping function.

To fulfill its social functions and promote social development, public relations needs to strengthen education and guidance to the public. Having completed these assignments will also improve the organization's reputation.

▶Two Directions of Cultivating Public Relations Consciousness

The cultivation of public relations consciousness is mainly manifested in the internal and external aspects.

Internally, the main function is to spread public relations awareness, ideas, skills, and update related knowledge.

Externally, the main function is to educate and guide the public. It is often said that "the public is always right", which is to give "right" to the other party from the perspective of service. However, objectively speaking, the public cannot always be right; they need to be guided.

In addition, with the rapid development of science and technology and the great abundance of products, public relations is needed to cultivate the market. It is impossible for the public to understand so many new products. Therefore, it is necessary to educate and guide them with commodity knowledge, correct consumption concept, safety insurance, etc., so as to make the consumer groups and organizations keep pace with each other.

Eliminate Risks and Crisis

Organizational crisis is the enemy of the survival and development of an organization. If not handled properly, it will cause heavy losses, and even "kill" the organization. Therefore, an organization should regard crisis management as one of the main functions and priorities of public relations. With the development of the theory and practice of public relations, forecasting risks and actively carrying out crisis management have become the mainstream methods to protect the organization's interests and image.

When an emergency or a major accident occurs, the public relations of an organization will be in a state of chaos, facing strong public opinion pressure from the environment. To handle the crisis events often requires the mobilization of the whole organization and the comprehensive use of various media, which make it a complex and special action based on the timely and sound public relations project.

►Investigation and Judgment of Crisis Events

After the occurrence of major crisis events, we should first use effective investigation methods to quickly figure out the situation, judge the nature, status, consequences and impact of the event, so as to lay a foundation for the response policies and emergency measures.

(1) Find out the nature and status of the incident: traffic accidents such as air crash, train derailment, and ship sinking; serious production and business accidents such as toxic pollution, fire and food poisoning; or life and property damage accidents caused by natural disasters. The time, place and reason of the incident, whether it has been controlled or is getting worse are also important elements.

(2) Identify the consequences and effects of the incident, such as the number of casualties, the economic losses, the extent and scope of other damages, and the social impact these consequences have and will have.

(3) Identify the public objects involved in the incident: people who are directly or indirectly injured; organizations or individuals who have direct or indirect responsibilities or interest relations with the incident itself; organizations related to the handling of the incident; and the media and public opinion circles, etc. Special attention should be paid to keeping in touch with the witnesses and dealing with the press relations carefully.

►Basic Principles for Handling Crisis Events

Crisis events are generally unexpected. Since the public opinion has a great influence, and the time is relatively urgent, it is usually difficult to deal with the crisis events perfectly. Within an organization, the public relations department is often in the front line. Its policies of decision-making and actions shall follow the BASIC principles:

(1) Balance the interests of the organization and the public to the maximum extent;

(2) Actively deal with the aftermath;

(3) Stabilize all parties, keep calm and judge the situation;

(4) Initiative should be strived for;

(5) Calm down, control the situation and try to recover from the influence.

In short, the purpose of public relations in dealing with crisis events is to "truly disperse and efface the bad influence". When a crisis event occurs, people related to it, out of the instinct of pursuing advantages and avoiding disadvantages, will strongly demand to understand the situation and their relationship with it. If there is no reliable information, they often make the worst assumption as the basis for their actions. Only true and accurate communication can win the understanding, trust, and cooperation from the public. Only when we guide the public opinion can we turn the unfavorable factors into favorable ones and restore the social reputation of the organization as soon as possible.

Learning to Practice

Scan to Read More

You are a member of the Environmental and Resource Protection Committee of the City People's Congress. The Environmental Health Bureau has announced a plan to build a garbage disposal site in the nearby countryside. The plan claims to have no impact on nearby residents and groundwater, but does not provide convincing any evidence. The opponents say the plan is too hasty and unscientific. Through field investigation, you find that this garbage disposal site will have little impact on the nearby residents and groundwater. After completion, it will greatly improve the urban garbage treatment capacity, improve the urban environment, and attract financial investment. How are you going to push the plan forward?

Indication for Answer

You could not refuse to take part in "propaganda" to convince the citizens that it is safe because you still believe it is a health threat. After this action, you put your opinion before facts and the best interest of your employer and the community. You need not immediately develop an action plan to persuade the citizens that it is in their best interest, or plan a year-long grass-root movement to change public opinion on the subject. If you do as this, you will jump to the second step of the four-step problem-solving process, skipping the first step. As a result, the actions taken could be ineffective or even counterproductive. Maybe you intend to ask the public relations practitioners in another city whose award-winning program secured public acceptance of a landfill to send you a copy of the PR plan. It is not acceptable because it ignores the major differences in time, place, and circumstance between your situation and theirs. Certainly, after you understand your situation in details, you might want to study the program to see what could be generalized from it. So first you have to conduct research to investigate various stakeholders' views and media habits, and then determine which is the best answer.

Case Study

Case 3.1 Bytedance Shows *Lost in Russia* on Streaming Sites for Free

▶ Replay of the Event

Chinese film *Lost in Russia* made history in becoming the first movie debuting during the Spring Festival of 2020 on streaming platforms for free.

TikTok's owner Bytedance, a growing Internet technology tycoon, reached an agreement with Huanxi Meida Group Limited to exclusively broadcast the latter's production *Lost in Russia* on its several platforms, including Douyin (the Chinese version of TikTok), Toutiao and Xigua Video.

Lost in Russia was one of the seven Chinese films originally planned to debut in Chinese mainland cinemas during the Spring Festival holidays of 2020 but joined the premiere cancellation announcement due to the concerns of coronavirus.

The news that *Lost in Russia* will be aired on streaming sites for free during the Spring Festival trended on China's Twitter-like Sina Weibo with a lot of netizens praising the innovative and bold decision of both the streaming platforms and the film's producers.

▶ Response

Huanxi Media Group Limited announced its intention to establish an all-around and strategic cooperation with Bytedance. Aside from paying for the broadcast rights of the films and dramas owned by Huanxi, Bytedance will also produce high-quality contents and explore to open a brand new streaming channel with Huanxi.

According to media reports, Bytedance made a payment of 630 million yuan ($90.83m) to broadcast Huanxi's contents on its platforms. Huanxi canceled its 2.4 billion yuan box-office income guarantee agreement with the investors of *Lost in Russia* due to the film not being able to debut in Chinese mainland cinemas. The agreement said that Huanxi could get its around 600 million yuan production fees only when the film earns over 2.4 billion yuan.

►Result

The shares of Huanxi Media Group Limited rose 43.07 percent to HK $1.96 as of Friday noon after the cooperation was revealed early in the morning.[1]

►Reflection

Bytedance' case has become one of the most classic public relations cases in 2020. The public relations team has a quick response and first-class execution. For enterprises, the focus of marketing is naturally on the line, especially social marketing. The epidemic situation is merciless, but the brand can still play a good public relations communication effect.

There are many ways to take advantage of the situation. The most important thing is that the speed of chasing hot spots should be fast, the posture should be correct, and the positive energy should be the first.

Case 3.2　Sleeping Phenomenon in IKEA Furniture Store

►Replay of the Event

In August 2019, some netizens disclosed that many people went to IKEA to enjoy free air conditioning in summer and sleep on IKEA's furniture. They thought that this was crowding out the public space of other customers and tarnishing the image of the store. Moreover, according to media reports, some customers in IKEA not only sit on the sofa, but also take off their shoes and sit cross legged, as if in their own living room.

►Response

On August 22, IKEA's president in China said that IKEA is very happy to see people come to IKEA for rest. IKEA hopes to create a place where people and friends can get together and give consumers a very pleasant experience.

►Result

Netizens praised IKEA's open and tolerant public relations. Netizens think that since the phenomenon has already happened and IKEA can't stop it, they should simply follow the trend, welcome and support users to experience, reflecting IKEA's generous and tolerant

---

① https://www.globaltimes.cn/content/1177812.shtml.

attitude. By this incident IKEA also launched a wave of free advertising for the enterprise's strategic online and offline shopping platform. As a happy result, IKEA's popularity in the hearts of netizens continues to rise, and netizens are more inclined to shop there.

► Reflection

With the rapid development of science and technology and the great abundance of products, which is impossible for the public to understand timely, the market needs cultivating through public relations. It is necessary to educate and guide the customers with commodity knowledge, correct consuming knowledge, safety insurance, etc., so as to make the consumer groups and organizations keep pace with each other. IKEA's Beijing branch once has begged shoppers to stop sleeping on the furniture four years ago, but now it changed.[①]

Case 3.3 Golden Rooster Award Folk Poster Competition

► Replay of the Event

On August 12, 2019, when the 28th China Jinji Baihua Film Festival (Golden Rooster and Hundred Flowers Film Festival) was about to be held, the famous design aesthetics blogger "Niyacaimeigong" launched a folk poster competition, calling for "Save This Rooster" and inviting netizens to design the festival's poster.

► Response

On August 13, the official Weibo account of Jinji Baihua Film Festival said, "Thank you all for supporting the China Golden Rooster and Hundred Flowers Film Festival. Thank you for your creativity and design! We will continue to work hard to do our job well. Thank you for coming with us all the way."

► Result

On October 22, the design of the main visual poster of the 28th China Golden Rooster and Hundred Flowers Film Festival was exposed. The aesthetic appreciation was recognized by the public as "progressive" and "not bad".

---

① HORTON H. IKEA in Beijing Has Begged Shoppers to Stop Sleeping on the Furniture[EB/OL]. [2021-4-5]. https://www.mirror.co.uk/usvsth3m/ikea-beijing-begged-shoppers-stop-5480150.

▶Reflection

The festival did not make complaints, but thanked the netizens for their creativity and design. It took advantage of the folk poster contest to publicize the event and improve the attention. The interaction times of this response blog post was also one of the tops in the whole year, and the netizens even left a message to encourage the domestic film festival "striving for success". At the same time, this response gave the netizens an image that is inclusive and close to people.

The fans once made complaints about the film festival in previous years. After the launch of the folk poster competition, the creation desire of the netizens was aroused. People actively participated in this activity, and a series of exquisite works with far-reaching implications have been produced, among which there were also some "playing with the fun" works.

Courseware   Quiz

Chapter 4
Practitioners and Organization—the Subject of Public Relations

Preparation for Start

Scan to Dialogue   Scan to Listen

If you have three years of public relations experience, you would have become very analytical from your previous job. And you will find that you are obliged to be more responsible and adaptable. At least, owing to your problem-solving skills, you could easily endure difficulties.

Understanding Objectives

After studying Chapter 4, you should be able to:

1. Set up a public relations department within an organization.

2. Hire public relations companies.

3. List main public relations associations in China.

4. Train practitioners of public relations.

Basic Concepts and Elements

Public relations activities are composed of three basic elements: the subject, the object, and the means. In a broad sense, the subject of public relations refers to any social organization that is purposefully and systematically constructed with specific functions, tasks, and social behavior abilities. In a narrow sense, the subject of public relations mainly refers to the institutions and personnel specialized in performing public relations functions. In an organization, the main function of public relations department is dissemination and communication. The public relations department plays a role of "margin" and "intermediary", that is, between the decision-making department and other professional functional departments, between the organization and the external environment, public relations undertakes the responsibilities of establishing contact, communicating information, providing consultation and suggestions, planning and programming, coordinating actions, and supporting services.

Setting up a Public Relations Department within an Organization

The main modes of setting up a public relations department within an organization are as follows:

(1) Subordinated type. The public relations department reports to sales department; or reports to advertising or publicity department; or reports to contact reception department; or reports to the administrative office.

(2) Parallel type. The public relations department is arranged in parallel with other functional departments of the organization.

(3) The public relations department directly reports to the top leaders, that is, it is in the third level of the whole organization system, lower than other functional departments. But it directly responds to the highest decision-making level and management level.

(4) Public relations committee. It is a public relations coordination committee led by the leaders in charge of the organization and jointly organized by the heads of various functional departments to guide and coordinate the overall PR activities, and an office will be set up to cope with daily work.

The characteristics of the public relations department in an organization are as follows: (1) understanding the internal situation; (2) facilitating coordination; (3) high efficiency; (4) low cost; (5) the work is restricted by the internal factors of the organization, so it is difficult to be absolutely objective and fair.

The public relations department established within an organization, like other departments, is an important functional department and plays a very important role. Its functions and takes are as follows.

(1) Collect information. The primary function of a public relations department in the information age is to collect, manage and disseminate information. The establishment of public relations department can strengthen the organization's social contact, and then build up a smooth informing network, which plays the role of "ears and eyes" of the organization.

(2) Plan the overall image engineering. The design of Corporate Identity System (CIS), the conception of organizational culture, the positioning of popularity and reputation, and the selection of various schemes should all be carefully planned. The public relations department can play the role of organization image engineer.

(3) Act as a decision-making adviser. While the public relations department should shape the image of the whole organization, it is not on the highest decision-making level, but the "think tank" and "brain trust" of the organization. It is also the environment

monitoring and trend forecasting center. It is responsible for providing a complete set of alternative decision-making schemes and assisting the organization in making decisions and strategies.

(4) Carry out publicity and liaison. In order to gain the perception, understanding and trust of the public, win the love, support and cooperation from the external world, an organization should constantly publicize itself to the public. The public relations department is the mouthpiece of the organization. With the development of market economy, organizations need to contact with foreign countries more and more closely, and the task of outward contact and communication becomes more and more important. At the same time, various frictions and disputes between organizations and the environment are also increasing, which requires coordination. In this regard, the public relations department is the "ministry of foreign affairs" of an organization.

Hiring Public Relations Companies

Public relations company refers to consulting companies and other independent public relations service agencies. A public relations company is composed of all kinds of PR experts and professionals. It is an information-based, intelligent and communication service unit that provides PR consultation for social organizations or accepts entrustment to carry out PR activities for customers. It stands for a fiduciary relationship between the public relations specialists and the organization the specialists serve for.

In January 1985, Hill+Knowlton Strategies, one of the largest international public relations companies based in the United States, set up an office in Beijing. In August 1985, Burson-Marsteller, an American public relations company signed a contract with China News Development Corporation to establish China Global Public Relations Company, which is the first professional public relations company in China.

The types of public relations companies include:

(1) It is divided into special events company, special service company and comprehensive service consulting company according to it's specialties.

Special events company is a company that provides some kind of public relations techniques and skills for customers' special events with various professionals, technologies and equipment.

Special service company provides public relations services for specific industries.

Comprehensive service consulting company can adapt to the needs of multi-industries, multi-functions and the whole process of public relations.

(2) It is divided into cooperative company and independent company according to the mode of operation.

Cooperative company is a kind of public relations company that cooperates with other advertising companies.

Independent company adheres to the uniqueness of its own business. Whether operating single, special, multiple or comprehensive business, it does not cooperate with advertising companies or other departments.

Large and medium-sized public relations companies are generally composed of the following parts: administrative department; planning and auditing department; professional techniques department; international and regional departments.

The business scope of a public relations company is as follows: (1) consultation and diagnosis; (2) liaison and communication; (3) information collection; (4) news agency; (5) advertising agency; (6) product promotion; (7) conference service; (8) planning activities; (9) concierge service; (10) printing production; (11) audio and video production; (12) training service.

The characteristics of public relations company services are: (1) objective and fair; (2) comprehensive technology and strong professionalism; (3) more flexible and adaptable; (4) distant relationship; (5) high operating cost.

There are several points to pay attention to when hiring a public relations consultant:

(1) Select a consultant with professional standards and good moral characters;

(2) Trust the consultant and provide it with true and accurate information;

(3) Maintain good communication and cooperation with the consultant; regularly invite the consultant to attend the situation analysis meeting and decision-making meeting;

(4) Respect the consultant's judgment, listen to the advice with an open mind, and give a detailed explanation of the rejection of the opinion;

(5) Prevention is better than cure, so employ consultants before problems and crises arise;

(6) The consultants should be relatively stable, because the tacit understanding between the two sides needs a period of running.

Public Relations Association

Public relations association is a professional organization in this field. It is a non-profit social organization. The establishment and development of trade associations is a sign of the maturity of public relations. The International Public Relations Association was founded in

1955 and Shanghai Public Relations Association was established in November 1986.

IPRA, the International Public Relations Association, is the leading global network for public relations professionals. Its members are individuals rather than corporates. It aims to further the development of open communication and the ethical practice of public relations. IPRA fulfils this aim through networking opportunities, maintaining code of conduct and providing intellectual leadership. IPRA is the organizer of the annual Golden World Awards for Excellence—the global awards scheme in PR. With 60 odd years of experience, IPRA, recognized by the United Nations, is now present throughout the world wherever public relations is practiced. IPRA welcomes all those within the profession who share its aim and who wish to be part of the IPRA worldwide fellowship.[①]

The main activities of the public relations association include: (1) contacting members; (2) compiling codes of ethics for the industry, and maintaining the image and reputation of the industry; (3) professional training; (4) popularizing knowledge; (5) editing and publishing publications.

In the early 1980s, modern public relations theories and practice were introduced into China with the Reform and Opening-up Policy. A group of pioneers devoted themselves in PR concept promoting, theory study and practice, meanwhile professional organizations and corporations were set up one after another.

China Public Relations Association (CPRA) was founded in 1987 in Beijing. It is composed of government departments, institutions, media, colleges, enterprises, experts, scholars and practitioners in the field of public relations. It is a non-profit social organization approved and registered by the Ministry of Civil Affairs.[②]

Since its establishment, CPRA has been committed to the development of China's public relations industry; it actively participated in international PR activities, carried forward the Chinese national culture, and proactively carried out industry self-discipline, resource integration, international exchange and cooperation, talent training, theoretical research and other aspects of work. The association has a large number of senior professors and experts at home and abroad. It cooperates with relevant organizations and famous colleges and universities all around the world to organize professional training and certification, compile professional books and teaching materials, and promote the overall quality of the industry.

---

① https://www. linkedin. com/organization-guest/company/international-public-relations-association-ipra? trk= organization-update_share-update_update-text&challengeId=AQF_skzArWkYwQAAAXOUYIBSdbag0X6 yyXWaeY4-FgsUAjEiwUQFbd_ThM0hfTl6ogGwP-FTT5_odoWqpoCvr4bDyFdizTruKQ&submissionId=b0b a3e73-cdda-2516-a574-26ead1749b4f.

② https://baike.baidu.com/item/中国公共关系协会/8712713?fr=aladdin.

Through holding various lectures and forums, the association provides timely information services for members and industries; by holding various activities, it promotes the mutual understanding among different parties, it also provides services for Chinese enterprises to enter the world and for overseas information, talents, technology and funds to enter China.[1]

China International Public Relations Association (CIPRA), set up in April 1991 as a corporate body and headquartered in Beijing, is a national organization aimed at international cooperation in the field of public relations. In 2007, CIPRA obtained the Special Consultative Status of ECOSOC. In 2009, CIPRA obtained "3A" level from the Ministry of Civil Affairs. Mr. Li Daoyu, the former ambassador of PRC to the United States, was elected as the first president of CIPRA. Ms. He Luli, Mr. Jiang Zhenghua, Mr. Cheng Siwei, Mr. Li Meng, Mr. Tomur Dawamat and Mr. Yuan Baohua are the honorary presidents of the association.[2]

In the past years, lots of local and multinational top enterprises as well as PR agencies have become CIPRA's corporate members. Many senior practitioners, experts and scholars have joined CIPRA as individual members. China Golden Awards for Excellence in Public Relations, China University Students Public Relations Contest, China International Public Relations Congress, China Public Relations Carnival, China Public Relations Industry Annual Survey Report, Public Relations Lectures and Training Program, and other professional activities have been facilitated by CIPRA. To foster the professionalization, standardization and internationalization of China's public relations business, CIPRA has done a lot of work in the National Test of Occupational Qualification of Public Relations Practitioners, and has been holding related working seminars annually, which are recognized and supported by the professionals in the circle.[3]

Public Relations Practitioners

Public relations practitioners include PR leaders and the general personnel.

PR leaders refer to the managers, directors and persons in charge of public relations departments in organizations. They are responsible for all aspects of PR activities, playing a core role in an organization. Their daily work includes:

(1) To determine work objectives and work plans;

---

[1] https://baike.baidu.com/item/中国国际公共关系协会/2958119?fr=aladdin.

[2] http://www.cipra.org.cn/templates/T_Content/index.aspx?nodeid=53.

[3] http://www.cipra.org.cn/templates/T_Content/index.aspx?nodeid=53.

(2) To budget and allocate human resource, funds, equipment and time;

(3) To lead all public relations personnel to carry out their work;

(4) To coordinate the relations among all parties through internal and external communication.

General public relations personnel includes: (1) investigation and analysis personnel (mainly responsible for evaluating the organization's image and the effect of work by the organization's public relations department, so as to find out the causes of the problems); (2) planners; (3) communicators; (4) secretaries; (5) specialized technical personnel (e.g., financial personnel).

The consciousness of public relations personnel includes: (1) image consciousness (this is the core); (2) service consciousness; (3) mutual benefit consciousness (utilitarian consciousness); (4) communication consciousness; (5) long-term consciousness; (6) innovation consciousness.

The psychological qualities of public relations personnel include: (1) self-confidence (the most basic requirement); (2) enthusiastic attitude; (3) open mind.

The knowledge structure of public relations personnel includes: (1) basic theoretical knowledge; (2) basic practical knowledge.

The basic abilities of public relations personnel include: (1) strong written and oral expressing ability; (2) well organizing ability; (3) sound thinking and planning ability; (4) keen observation ability; (5) well self-controlling and flexible adaptability; (6) strong communicating ability; (7) mastering policies and theories.

Training of Public Relations Practitioners

Public relations practitioners can be trained for two goals: The first is for PR leaders, focusing on the all-round ability of management, planning and communication; the second is for the general PR personnel, focusing on the cultivation of professional techniques, skills and crafts.

The training for public relations practitioners can be carried out not only through undergraduate education and postgraduate education, but also through various continuing education, and training classes held for all staff. It is worth mentioning that the training for the whole staff can enhance their public relations consciousness, improve their public relations behavior, strengthen their coordination and initiative, so as to form a strong atmosphere and vivid culture of public relations.

The training for public relations practitioners should follow the following principles: (1) combining scientific theoretical knowledge with ideological and moral education; (2) combining theory with practice; (3) teaching according to the characteristics of different personnel and different teaching materials; (4) combining professional knowledge with comprehensive knowledge.

Public relations practitioners must have the following practical working abilities:

(1) Organizing ability. Public relations practitioners often have to organize various types of PR activities, so their organizing ability is required. The organizing ability is mainly manifested in the process of organizing meetings, press conference, marketing exhibition, achievement exhibition, etc., implementing plans and effectively eliminating the uncontrollable factors. To ensure the maximum realization of objectives, public relations work should be carried out continuously. In a word, making the PR activities complete and orderly without mistakes is one of the basic skills for a practitioner to master.

(2) Expression ability. The expression ability includes written expression and oral expression. Being able to speak and write are two basic requirements for public relations practitioners. Speaking, including speech, conversation, negotiation, etc., is a common working method used by public relations practitioners; writing includes writing various press releases, organizing various official documents, designing advertising words, sorting out publicity materials, and writing speeches or reports. Public relations practitioners must have solid ink skills. A public relations practitioner who can't write is missing a hand. The public relations departments of some foreign organizations regard "being good at writing" as the first professional requirement, which shows the importance of writing skills. The cultivation of writing ability is not achieved overnight. It requires public relations practitioners to have a certain cultural literacy and writing foundation, and then adhere to practice, so as to make progress. As public relations practitioners deal with people, they must have the ability of oral expression. When a person's oral ability is strong enough to produce the magic effect of attracting, moving, persuading and giving people a good impression, he may achieve the ideal effect that PR practitioners often expect. In terms of expression ability, in addition to mastering the language of one's motherland, PR practitioners should also have the ability of foreign language communication. In the meantime, they could use non-verbal expressions like movements, clothing, etc., to express a certain meaning, and even the control of time and space to express what the verbal means cannot convey.

(3) Social ability. Social ability is the ability to contact and communicate with the public. It is also the basic condition for public relations practitioners to make good connections and relations among all parties, and strive for public understanding and support. Only when a public relations practitioner has strong social skills, can he seize the opportunity in any occasion, make friends widely and be welcomed by others, so as to create a favorable interpersonal environment for his work. In social communication, public relations practitioners must understand the etiquette, habits and customs of various countries and regions. They

must determine their own conversation content, style and behavior according to the level of education, nationality, gender, age and identity of the communication objects, and avoid undesirable speech or impolite behaviors.

(4) Adaptability. Some unexpected events or problems often appear in public relations work. In the face of these questions, public relations practitioners should keep calm, quickly find out the cause, make correct judgment and put forward appropriate countermeasures. The more difficult the situation is, the more confident a mature public relations practitioner should be. They need to be good at mobilizing all the favorable factors either objective or subjective in difficult situations, so that they can gradually get out of the crisis and solve the problems satisfactorily.

(5) Innovation ability. The field of public relations is very extensive, which provides an ideal environment for practitioners to display their imagination and talents. They should be good at catching new information, enhancing new knowledge, establishing new ideas, putting forward new concepts, daring to innovate, skillfully conceiving some novel and unique forms of activities, so as to carry out PR work vividly, full of energy and vigor.

(6) Good professional ethics. All walks of life have their own moral standards, and the public relations industry is no exception. The practitioners must abide by the standards of professional ethics, in order to obtain the career development in this industry. In some countries, many perfect professional ethics have been formulated. For example, the code of professional ethics of the International Public Relations Association (adopted in 1965), the professional ethics of the American Public Relations Association, etc. China's public relations cause started relatively late, and there is no universally recognized standard of professional ethics. On September 27, 1989, the Second Joint Meeting of Provincial and Municipal Public Relations Organizations proposed the draft and implementation plan of China's code of ethics for public relations, which is based on China's socially recognized moral standards and the domestic conditions. Although it needs to be further improved, its birth is undoubtedly a great development in the history of China's public relations.

In a word, public relations practitioners should be specialized in the investigation, consultation, planning and implementation of public information dissemination, relationship coordination and image management of organizations. At the same time, they should abide by the following moral norms in their work: (1) fair; (2) decent; (3) responsible for the society; (4) truthful (the lifeline of public relations work); (5) confidential.

Learning to Practice

Scan to Read More

A private university is about to celebrate its 40th anniversary. The president decided to set up a public relations department and hire a vice president to deal with the matter. The president hopes that the department can help the university establish a good relationship with various media and do a good job in the publicity work.

The president expects the new deparpment to produce monthly bulletin for community and alumni groups, and run the university's websites, blogs, WeChat official account and short video accounts. Of course, these things can also be finished through employing specialized public relations companies. What are the pros and cons of adding an employee and hiring a public relations company?

Indication for Answer

1. Of the activities that the president wants done in the extended function, you may recommend an outside firm should manage the annual special event, which is not necessary on a full-time and prolonged basis. Handling the regular press relations and producing publicity for university programs relate to on-going PR work. They require staff attention throughout the year. Producing monthly newsletters and running the university's website require both graphic design and desktop publishing skills, which will be practiced more frequently than the management skills needed to implement the anniversary.

2. If you owned a local public relations firm, you may give him the best reason for hiring an outside agency. Since your firm is in the same city as the university, it isn't applicable that you suggest the geographical scope of operations of your firm. Obviously, objectivity, flexibility and prior experience are all good reasons, but not the best.

Case Study

PUBLIC RELATIONS

Case 4.1 Bilibili Supports Jing Hanqing

▶Replay of the Event

Jing Hanqing (敬汉卿) is a famous Vlogger at the video sharing website, Bilibili (also called Website B). He had 6.62 million followers as of October 30, 2019.

On August 3, 2019, Jing Hanqing posted a video saying that his account had been registered as a trademark by "Zhiqiao Electronic Products Sales Department of Jinghu District" and they asked him to change his name, which attracted attention of netizens. The video rapidly became viral and triggered extensive discussions—this may explain why he has become an icon in the fight against malicious trademark applications.

In May 2018, a trademark application was filed by Zhiqiao Electronic Products Sales Department ("Zhiqiao") in class 41 for services of entertainment, video production and downloading (application no. 31259902). The application was approved on February 28, 2019. This looked like just another "normal" trademark squatting story, at least until August 2019, when Jing Hanqing received a "trademark infringement notice" sent by Zhiqiao.

The notice asked Jing Hanqing, in an unquestionable tone, to stop infringing the "敬汉卿" trademark registration. In other words, Jing Hanqing must stop using his own name on all media, including WeChat and Weibo, or Zhiqiao would enforce its exclusive trademark rights. [①]

Unlike other peacemakers, Jing did not follow the usual procedures. Instead, he posted a video and ranted to an audience of millions.

▶Response

Subsequently, netizens burst out that the well-known uploader "Xiangxiang Battle" and the official accounts of Website B such as "Waiguoren Research Association" were also found to have been reported infringement. Even the account of Sina Weibo CEO has been

---

① China Introduces New Regulation Tackling Bad Faith Trademarks... and Who Is Jing Hanqing?〔EB/ OL〕. 〔2021-4-20〕. https://ipstork.com/china-introduces-new-regulation-tackling-bad-faith-trade-marks-and-who-is-jing-hanqing/.

registered as a trademark of sex goods. At the same time, netizens dig out that Zhiqiao Electronics has accumulated 109 registered trademarks in a short period of time since 2017, of which there are many media bloggers' names.

▶Result

On August 6, 2019, Website B responded that it would not ask the uploader to modify its nickname because it was maliciously preempted by other organizations, and would provide corresponding legal assistance for the uploaders. In the future, it would also launch the "Uploaders Creative Rights and Interests Protection Plan" to provide more professional and three-dimensional legal support. For the "auxiliary attack" of Bilibili and the "maintenance" of uploaders, netizens have expressed their approval and strongly support the rights protection.

The strong pressure from public opinion drove Zhiqiao to eventually withdraw the said trademark registration.

As a key point of Chinese government's initiative to curb the proliferation of malicious trademark applications, Several Provisions for Regulating Application for Trademark Registration (规范商标申请注册行为若干规定, hereinafter referred to as "the Provisions") has gone into effect as of December 1, 2019. The full text has been published on the China National Intellectual Property Administration official website.[①]

▶Reflection

Like values, professional ethics provide rules on how a person should act towards other people and institutions in such an environment. Professional ethics are principles that govern the behaviour of a public relations practitioner or a consulting firm in a business environment.

Case 4.2 Dismantled Meizu 16S: SOC Is Not Sealed

▶Replay of the Event

At 19:00 on May 7, 2019, XYZONE, a science and technology evaluation company, released a video entitled "Dismantled Meizu 16S: SOC Is Not Sealed yet" on its Weibo account, causing a great stir. SOC (system on a chip) being not sealed with glue means once the mobile phone is wet by water, there is no way to repair it. People from all walks of life doubted that Meizu 16S had "cut corners".

---

① *Ibid.*

▶Response

At 23:00 on May 7, Meizu Care responded that the new glue "Fule 8023" was applied, which could reduce the glue coverage on the edge of the chip with better permeability, and made the motherboard more beautiful.

However, when it was close to 1:00 on May 8, Weibo account "Lou Bin XYZONE" said that it was obvious in the video that there was no glue sealing measures for the Meizu 16S SOC. This mobile phone is a retail version purchased from the official website. After the incident was exposed, some netizens called on Meizu to add glue and then deliver the product.

Meizu CEO Huang Zhang responded forcefully that if someone takes the phone apart and finds no glue, he will pay for two sets as compensation.

▶Result

At 0:00 on May 9, "Lou Bin XYZONE" said that Meizu officials went to his company on the afternoon of May 8 to investigate and solve the Meizu 16S glue sealing incident. Meizu engineer confirmed on site that the 16S XYZONE kept had a very few leakage points in the assembly line. They compensated XYZONE with two Meizu 16S phones and repaired the original one.

▶Reflection

After the first round of response from both sides, XYZONE confirmed that Meizu 16S did not have glue dispensing, which led to a significant rise in negative emotions; after Huang Zhang said "one for two", positive emotions began to rise; later "Lou Bin XYZONE" confirmed that Meizu had acknowledged the problem and offered compensation, and the positive emotions soared. This shows that Meizu's public relations crisis-solving scheme is relatively successful. Huang Zhang dares to face up to the problem, and the company is able to make a promise. These two steps make Meizu's "craftsman spirit" not collapse, and get good results.

Case 4.3 "Can't Afford Peiling Mustard"

▶Replay of the Event

On the morning of August 8, 2019, a blogger disclosed that "now we can't even afford to eat pickled mustard". The screenshot of a program in Taiwan was used in the blog image. A spokesman for the program concluded that people in the Chinese mainland couldn't even afford to eat pickled mustard because the share price of Fuling mustard plummeted. Subsequently, Weibo account "Headline News" and "Observer Net" and other media influencers forwarded the news, which quickly attracted the attention of netizens. "Can't afford Fuling pickled mustard" is nonsense in the eyes of netizens. The spokesman's remark ignored the facts and caused people's ridicule and banter.[1]

▶Response

On the evening of August 8, the account "Fuling Pickle in Wujiang" launched a Weibo lottery in response to the hot topic: "Can't afford it, we send it!" At the same time, netizens corrected the pronunciation of the controversial spokesperson: "It's Fuling, not Peiling!"

▶Result

In one day, forwarding number of the lottery reached 100,000+, which has set a new record compared with the amount of interactive blog posts published at ordinary times.

In terms of the number of participants, the event was a great success. Many netizens joked that since they "can't afford it", they can only rely on other people's giving.

▶Reflection

Taking "sending" as the key word, the lucky draw of Fuling pickled mustard successfully grasped the hot topic, narrowed the distance with netizens, and established the reputation image of the enterprise. Also, the public opinion reached a peak on August 8 and 9 with the company's stock price and turnover rate increasing.

The primary function of public relations department in social media age is still to collect, manage and disseminate information. "Fuling Pickle in Wujiang", as a branch of the public relations department in the corporate, strengthened the social contact, and then established a smooth informing network, which played an effective role as "ears and eyes" of the organization.

Courseware   Quiz

---

[1] https://zhuanlan.zhihu.com/p/77730089.

Chapter 5

Public—the Object of Public Relations

Preparation for Start

In the retail industry, customer service is important for public relations and marketing. It is also very important in developing and maintaining customer relations. Customer service is significant in keeping business flowing, and it even determines the long-term Development of any business.

Understanding Objectives

After studying Chapter 5, you should be able to:

1. Understand the main types of the public.
2. Master the main methods of dealing with the external public.
3. Define public opinion.

Basic Concepts and Elements

The object of public relations is called the public. The public refers to the total number of individuals, groups or organizations that are related to the interests of the organization— the public relations subject. The public and the organization interact with each other, that is, the public is the target object of PR communication activities. Five characteristics of the public are described as: (1) group; (2) commonality; (3) diversity; (4) variability; (5) correlation. There are different types of the public.

Several Types of the Public

According to where the objects are based, it can be divided into internal public and external public. The internal public refers to the objects of communication within the organization, including the groups composed of all members of the organization, such as management personnel, technical personnel, sales personnel, auxiliary personnel and shareholders. The external public refers to the objects of communication outside the organization, such as consumers, collaborators, competitors, journalists, and celebrities.

According to the importance of the relationship, it can be divided into primary public and secondary public. The primary public refers to the part that is related to the survival of the organization and determines the success or failure of the organization. The secondary public refers to the part that has a certain impact on the survival and development of the organization, but not decisive significance.

According to the stability of the relationship, it can be divided into temporary public, periodic public and stable public. The temporary public refers to the objects that formed due to a temporary factor, accidental event or special activity. The periodic public refers to the objects that appear according to certain laws and cycles, such as the peak of tourists on holidays, the candidates and parents in the entrance examination. The stable public refers to the objects with stable structure relationships. The division of temporary public, periodic public and stable public is the basis for formulating temporary countermeasures, periodic policies and stable policies of public relations.

According to the public's attitude towards the organization, it can be divided into the agreeable public, the adverse public and the marginal public. The agreeable public, or the compliant public, refers to the objects who have the approval intention and supportive attitude towards the policies, behaviors and products of the organization. The adverse public, or the public contrary to the will of the organization, refers to the objects who have negative intention and opposition to the policies, behaviors and products of the organization. The marginal public refers to the objects who hold an intermediate attitude towards the organization and whose views and intentions are not clear.

According to the value orientation of the organization, it can be divided into the popular public, the unpopular public and the pursued public. The popular public refers to the objects that fully meet the needs of the organization and actively express interest and intention to the organization. The unpopular public refers to the objects that violate the interests and wishes of the organization and pose potential or additional pressure and burden on the organization. The pursued public refers to the objects who conform to the interests and needs of the organization, but are not interested in the organization and lack communication willingness.

According to the different stages of public development, it can be divided into nonpublic, potential public, aware public and action public. Nonpublic refers to the objects which have nothing to do with the organization, whose views, attitudes and behaviors are not affected by the organization, and do not exert any effect on the organization. Potential public refers to the unseen, latent or future objects that come into being for the potential PR work. Aware public refers to those who have already known their own situations. They clearly realize that the problems they are facing are related to specific organizations and they need to know relevant information urgently, so they turn to the organizations for relevant rights and interests. Active public refers to the objects that have taken practical actions. They put pressure on the organization and force the organization to take corresponding actions.

The Importance of the Internal Public

The internal public is the main body to form the organizational strength, the main force for the organization to create first-class products, and the positive factor for shaping and promoting the image of the organization.

The internal public is the most important and actively productive factor in an organization. The main goal of internal public relations is to cultivate the sense of ownership.

In dealing with internal public relations, you should be able to:

(1) Establish the idea of "internal public first" and correctly understand the master status of the internal public in the organization;

(2) Strengthen dissemination and communication to enhance the democratic participation consciousness of the internal public;

(3) Carry out colorful activities and emotional investment;

(4) Be good at ideological work and cultivate the loyalty of the internal public.

Main Types of the External Public

▶ Informal Groups

The so-called informal group is a group which is formed naturally without official regulations to meet individual needs and desires. Informal groups are formed on the basis of friendship, same hobbies, colleagues, self-protection and mutual benefit, and so on.

The characteristics of informal groups are:

(1) They are formed spontaneously on the basis of similar psychological characteristics and common mental needs;

(2) They implement emotional logic with feelings as the cohesive link and the common attitudes towards the group as the value standards;

(3) The groups have strong overall awareness and pressure, and there are unwritten

norms, which have great binding force on the behavior of the members;

(4) There are naturally-formed leaders within the group, whose prestige is high and influence is great;

(5) There are relatively sensitive information transmission channels in the group, and the ideological communication among members is deep and smooth; and

(6) They have dual functions.

When dealing with different informal groups, we should take different actions:

(1) For positive informal groups, we should adopt the principle of support and protection;

(2) For intermediate informal groups, we should be cautious and pay attention to guiding them;

(3) For negative informal groups, we should take necessary measures to prevent further qualitative change or even deterioration. The general principle is education and transformation.

►Community Public

Community public refers to the objects in the community where the organization is located, which includes local authority management departments, local associate, residents and other social organizations.

The community public is so important for an organization that:

(1) The community can provide sufficient labor resources for the development of the organization. Community relation is the extension of the employee relations within an organization.

(2) The community can provide the organization with electricity, hydraulic energy, land and raw material resources.

(3) The community can provide the organization with social services such as transportation, security, environmental protection, shops, baths, schools, markets, etc.

(4) The community can provide the organization with direct environment for its survival and development, and the community also has sufficient purchasing power, which is a relatively stable market.

In dealing with community relations we should pay attention to:

(1) Strengthening the dissemination and communication of information to enhance understanding;

(2) Caring about and supporting community construction;

(3) Participating in and subsidizing various social public welfare activities.

▶Customer Public

Customer public refers to the buyers and consumers. The customer public can be divided into material consumers (including consumers of material goods, means of production, and means of consumption), and spiritual consumers (including audience of radio, television, cinema; readers of newspapers and books, etc.).

Why is the customer public important in the PR work? Three factors may be included for your consideration:

(1) The customer public is the sustenance of the organization;

(2) Good customer public relations can bring benefits to the organization;

(3) The customer public can help the organization establish the correct business purpose and continuously improve the service.

A practitioner may be called an artist if he deals with the customer relations as the following:

(1) Establishing the idea of serving the public and the concept of "customers are God";

(2) Meeting the needs of customers and providing high-quality products;

(3) Providing first-class services to the customers by thinking what they think and being concerned about the public;

(4) Properly handling disputes with customers.

Last but not least, disputes or conflicts with customers may erupt if:

(1) The material interests of customers are damaged;

(2) The spiritual interests of customers are damaged;

(3) The customer itself is in a bad mood;

(4) Customers are deliberately provocative.

The skills of handling disputes with customers mainly include:

(1) Mastering the first-hand information to find out the real causes of the disputes;

(2) Drawing up a treatment plan;

(3) Adopting the "cold treatment" tactics as much as possible if time permits;

(4) Implementing the related strategy as soon as possible.

▶Media Public

Media public refers to news and communication institutions and their staff with the characteristics of intermediary and object integration.

The significance of doing a good job in the relationship with the media public includes:

(1) Good media public relations can crystalize good public opinion;

(2) Good media public relations are conducive to the realization of large-scale and long-distance communication.

The principles of dealing with media public relations correctly consist of 4 dos and 4 don'ts:

(1) Do treat each other with courtesy;

(2) Do treat each other with sincerity and seek truth from facts;

(3) Do treat each other equally;

(4) Do treat each other with patience.

(5) Don't be wishful;

(6) Don't consider profits only;

(7) Don't exchange for oneself in disguise;

(8) Don't dig wells until you are thirsty.

▶ Government Public

Government public refers to government organs and their internal staff.

The importance of government public relations:

(1) Good government public relations can form favorable political, legal and social management environment for organizations;

(2) Good government public relations can make organizations obtain agreeable environment and get support in human, finance, material and information resources;

(3) Good government public relations can help organizations obtain suitable public opinion environment.

The principles of dealing with the government public include:

(1) Take the initiative to establish and strengthen the two-way communication with the relevant government departments;

(2) Consciously accept the government's control and guidance, and consciously undertake the responsibilities and obligations to the state and society;

(3) Be familiar with the specific settings, division of responsibilities and corresponding personnel to ensure the effective work;

▶ Celebrity Public

Celebrity public refers to those who have great influence on and appeal to public opinion and social life.

In order to establish a good relationship with celebrities, a practitioner should have in mind the following aspects:

(1) The knowledge and expertise of celebrities;

(2) Their social networks;

(3) Their social prestige.

In order to do a good job in the relationship with celebrities, we must pay attention to:

(1) Adhering to mutual benefits;

(2) The opportunity of communication;

(3) Strengthening the cultural cultivation of PR personnel.

▶ International Public

International public means that when an organization's products, personnel and activities enter the international scope, it will have an impact on the public of other countries, so that the organization needs to understand and adapt to the public environment of the target country.

The significance of doing well in international public relations includes:

(1) Serving the opening-up policy;

(2) Using cross-cultural communication means to promote the internationalization of the organization image.

To carry out international public relations activities, we should pay attention to the following two points:

(1) Carefully study and respect the political, economic, legal, institutional, historical and cultural status, moral norms, local customs, language expression habits, lifestyle and values of the target country, and design communication programs and implement public relations plans according to varied situations.

(2) Understand the public's influence on the organization's products and services, and properly handle their complaints. The design of products and company names should be acceptable to the public of the target country, and their interests and taboos in culture, customs, politics and religion should not be violated.

Public Opinion

Splitting "public opinion" into its two components, *public* and *opinion*, is perhaps the best way to understand the concept. Simply defined, public signifies a group of people who share a common interest in a specific subject. An opinion is the expression of an attitude on a particular topic.

Opinion is the language expression of attitude, and any opinion contains three components: (1) cognitive component; (2) emotional component; (3) volitional component.

Public opinion is the collective opinion of many people on some issues, problems, etc., especially as a guide to action, decision, or the like.[①] Public opinion is the common belief of all members of the society or the majority of people, and it is a kind of resonance after people communicate with each other. The press, radio and television are important in the formation of public opinion. They are often called barometers of public opinion. Public opinion includes at least four factors: (1) an issue; (2) a majority of individuals to express their opinions on this issue; (3) some consistency among these opinions; (4) direct or indirect influence of the consensus.

The characteristics of public opinion are: (1) certainly approved and supported by the majority of people; (2) always involving the problem of social peace and happiness; (3) containing rationality; (4) being effective; (5) generally not the opinion of the government. If it is, it will appear in the form of government announcement, declaration and policy.

There are three basic elements of public opinion: (1) the person or event as the object; (2) the public as the subject; (3) the opinion as the phenomenon.

There are four forms of public opinion: (1) social events; (2) social problems; (3) social conflicts; (4) social movements.

The "public" in "public opinion" has the following characteristics: (1) having common topics; (2) participating in the discussion process; (3) being spontaneous and loose; (4) having certain sequence.

A practitioner of public relations should pay attention to three functions of public opinion: (1) restriction and supervision; (2) encouragement; (3) guidance of people's views.

Learning to Practice

PUBLIC RELATIONS

Scan to Read More

You are responsible for the public relations work of a 40-year-old private university.

Recently, someone reported on the Internet that there is a special professor in your university who has forged his diploma. He has taken the higher education, but he does not have a postgraduate degree or a doctor's degree. The school thought he was a doctor and hired him as a professor. He has taught many courses, and his lectures are wonderful and popular with students. At present, we have not received any report of his violation of teachers' ethics. The teaching performance assessment is also excellent. In the face of the report, he admitted that he had forged his diploma. How will you respond to the report?

---

① https://www.dictionary.com/browse/public-opinion.

Indication for Answer

1. Dismiss the teacher.

2. Contact the news media such as websites, admit the facts and condemn such impostors.

3. Reflect on the relevant work of the school to prevent such things from happening again.

Case Study

Case 5.1 Burger King Drops Chopsticks Ad after Accusations of Cultural Insensitivity

▶Replay of the Event

In early April 2019, Burger King advertised a new hamburger on Instagram, in which the actors struggled to eat a hamburger with a pair of giant chopsticks. The images were suspected of being mischievous, which caused netizens' dissatisfaction and accusing Burger King of racial discrimination.[1]

▶Response

Burger King quickly responded to a growing public opinion crisis by removing the video from social media. "We are very sorry for this advertisement that offended (Asian) communities," said Woodbridge, head of marketing at the company. "It does not reflect our brand values of diversity and inclusiveness."[2]

---

[1] Burger King Drops Chopsticks Ad after Accusations of Cultural Insensitivity [EB/OL]. [2021-4-30]. https://www.bilibili.com/read/cv2418917.

[2] *Ibid*.

▶Result

Before the incident, the Italian brand D&G insulted the Chinese people with an ad similar in the style. After the Burger King incident, the media took the initiative to compare them. Many media spontaneously reported Burger King's follow-up behavior. In comparison with D&G, Burger King's public relations behavior has been well received.

▶Reflection

To carry out international public relations activities, we need to design communication programs and implement public relations plans according to the respective situations in different countries. Burger King's timely apology and removal of the video advertisement won an opportunity for itself, which made the incident not further ferment, and avoided further side impact on the public opinion.

Case 5.2 Wangbaobao Cereal Uses Opinion Leaders for Marketing

▶Replay of the Event

Wangbaobao, a cereal company began to search for up-loaders with a certain number of fans in Tiktok, Bilibili and other platforms that young people like, which accounted for a high frequency of advertising. Especially during the "Double 11" shopping carnival in 2019, the frequency of Wangbaobao's advertisement recommended by the up-loaders on Bilibili website was very high, and Wangbaobao was called a "whole network advertising campaigner".

▶Response

Wangbaobao's marketing team said they are keen to find "waist KOL" for advertising. The reason is: Compared with the top online influencers, the cooperation price of KOL in the middle is much lower; most of them are new consumers themselves, and they transmit the content to the audience, which is more likely to stimulate the continuous spread like tap water. They also said that they are very confident in the quality of their products and that it is timely to introduce preferential measures and a variety of new taste products during the "Double 11" shopping carnival.

▶Result

Wangbaobao is really well-known among young people. On the night of November 11, 2019, Wangbaobao defeated Quaker Instant Oats and other traditional cereal brands, winning top 1 of Tmall's cereal market, and completed the 10 million yuan angel round of financing. The performance in 2020 was also very impressive, with several hundred million yuan of C round financing completed in early December.

▶ Reflection

The success of Wangbaobao lies in:

The choice of advertising on the platforms where young people are active shows that its main target is the young generation. Choosing small and medium-sized uploaders to do the promotion bring its product image closer to the people. Wangbaobao has also launched new products continuously to attract youngsters.

Wangbaobao's defect is that the price of the product is slightly too high. There have been buyers complaining about that. Also, too many advertisements can somewhat arouse people's disgust.

Case 5.3 Jingdong Finance App Involved in User Privacy Infringement

▶ Replay of the Event

In the early morning of February 16, 2019, a netizen released a video that disclosed the Jingdong Finance App automatically saved the user's pictures in the Android phone folder, and questioned that the Jingdong Finance App violated the user's privacy. After the spread of media, the matter was quickly known by netizens, and the voice denouncing Jingdong Finance App was dominant.

▶ Response

On the afternoon of the same day, Weibo account "Jingdong Finance" responded to the questions raised by netizens, saying Jingdong Finance would never collect any information without the authorization of users, let alone stealing users' privacy. If the user opens the Jingdong Finance App and takes a screenshot, the App side will believe that the user may want to complain or suggest to the customer service. As long as the user does not take the initiative to send anything to customer service, the background system cannot see any private information.

The informants once again raised their own doubts: Jingdong Finance would also "steal" the photos of the camera taken by Make-up Mode. This has nothing to do with the "screenshot feedback" feature. How to explain it? From a technical point of view, the "screenshot feedback" function only needs to cache the original path of the image, and does not need to copy an original one.

On February 17, the official Weibo account of Jingdong issued a further statement of apology, saying that after the investigation, they first put forward the causes of the problem, and then suggested three improvement measures. It was found that the problem existed in the version 5.0.5 on Android system, and the application would be removed from the App store for modification.

▶Result

Some netizens accepted Jingdong Finance's apology, believing that they saw sincerity and responsibility in the statement. Some technology experts have come forward to verify the cause of the bug of Jingdong Finance. Just as the official explanation shows, there is no malice.

▶Reflection

If the material or spiritual interests of customers are damaged, conflicts or disputes may break out. It is rare to face the conflict just based on fact that the customer's own mood is not good or the customers are deliberately provocative. After Jingdong Finance apologized based on the serious research, the proportion of negative emotions decreased, while the proportion of positive and neutral emotions increased.

Courseware   Quiz

Chapter 6
Public Relations Planning

Preparation for Start

Scan to Dialogue Scan to Listen

As an important task of enterprise management, public relations planning is the key to shaping the image and gaining the success of an organization. You can set a short-term goal when you begin to work in a new organization, which is to get as much experience as possible. After that, you may undertake more leadership role. For example, within five years, you expect to make a promotion to district manager.

Understanding Objectives

After studying Chapter 6, you should be able to:

1. Understand the principles of public relations planning.

2. Understand the contents of public relations planning.

3. Master the main thinking methods of public relations planning.

4. Complete a copywriting of public relations planning.

Basic Concepts and Elements

Public relations planning can also be understood as making suggestions, drafting resolutions, or making proposals, which is the process for PR personnel to analyze the conditions and design the best action plan or program according to the target image requirements of the organization.

The characteristics of public relations planning are: (1) objective; (2) ideological; (3) creative; (4) procedural; (5) flexible; (6) time-efficient.

Public relations planning, as the primary task of high-level managers and the basis of decision-making, plays a vitally important role in the innovation of enterprise management.

Principles of Public Relations Planning

In the public relations planning activities, we must follow certain guiding principles and rules of action. The principles of public relations planning include "5S":

1. Sake

"For the sake of interest" should be the motive force of public relations planning and behavior. The interests of an organization consist of its economic and social benefits. In the planning of public relations, the first thing to consider is the public interest, because interest can stimulate the public to germinate desire and impulse, form interest concern and interest awareness, and then produce a sustained group of interest objectives.

2. Subjective-objectivity

It means that in the process of public relations planning and operation, planners should consciously and actively conform to the objective reality through various efforts.

3. System

It means that in the public relations planning, the activities should be considered as a system, and the planning and operation should be carried out according to the logic and frame of the system.

4. Science

It means that the planning scheme can be implemented and achieve scientific and effective results. For that reason, specific requirements of feasibility are included in the public relations planning: (1) feasibility analysis; (2) feasibility test; (3) action and effectiveness of the scheme.

5. Strategy

Planning is a kind of strategy, not limited to a specific step, including many tactics or measures. In the process of planning, planners should strive to look at the world from a dynamic perspective and think of countermeasures with a flexible mind, and the final scheme must have been considered with elasticity.

Main Contents of Public Relations Planning

Main contents of public relations planning can be concluded in six steps:

(1) Identify the objective;

(2) Design the theme;

(3) Analyze the target public;

(4) Select the media;

(5) Prepare the budget;

(6) Examine and approve the scheme.

It is an indispensable step for public relations personnel to determine the general objectives and specific objectives, because objectives are not only the basis for guiding and coordinating PR work, but also the standard for evaluating the implementation effect of the plan.

Public relations objectives are generally divided into four categories: (1) long-term objectives; (2) short-term objectives; (3) general objectives; and (4) special objectives.

In order to determine the objectives of public relations, we should have in mind that the objectives are to be clear, specific, feasible and controllable.

The target public should be analyzed according to the activity goal, the organization strength, and the needs of the organization.

The contents of public relations budget include: (1) expense budget; (2) human resource budget; (3) time budget.

Public relations budget preparation methods include:

(1) Sales volume extraction method (that is, the enterprise extracts a certain percentage of its planned annual sales volume as the budget expense).

(2) Project operation comprehensive method (that is, list the enterprise image project plans and the cost details and amount required for each plan, and verify the individual planning activity budget; then summarize the budget of each image planning project in the year, and finally get the conclusion).

(3) Average development speed prediction method (that is, use historical data to calculate the total and average development speed of the actual expenditure of corporate image building, and determine the budget amount of planning activities).

The Thinking Mode of Public Relations Planning

Creative planning method and expert planning method are the main thinking modes of public relations planning.

1. Creative Planning Method

(1) Theoretical thinking, which is based on scientific theory and professional knowledge;

(2) Image thinking, which means that planners select, analyze and synthesize the elements they need according to various phenomena in life;

(3) Intuitive thinking, of which the most commonly used form is associative thinking.

Associative thinking refers to the way in which planners associate one thing with another.

2. Expert Planning Method

It is a method to put forward opinions and carry out comprehensive analysis with the help of experts' creative logical thinking. By organizing experts in various fields with professional knowledge and experience to conduct comprehensive analysis and research on the status and development process of the planning object, a planner can find out its law and rules, so as to give a scientific and accurate assessment. This method is based on not only personal judgment, but also group brainstorming.

The characteristics of the individual judgment planning method can be described as it maximizes the micro intelligent organization effect of experts, makes full use of personal creativity, and at the same time, makes the respondents free from the influence of external environment, so as to avoid psychological pressure.

Group brainstorming method is also known as expert meeting planning method. Compared with individual judgment planning method, it has the following characteristics:

(1) It can give full play to the macro intelligent structure effect of a group consisting of several experts, and this effect is often greater than the sum of the individual creative ability of each member in the group;

(2) Through the information exchange among multiple experts, it can lead to thinking resonance and achieve gratifying creative results in a short time;

(3) The effect of the expert meeting is more than that of the group, and the amount of information is larger than that of any single member;

(4) The factors considered by the expert meeting are always more than those considered by a member alone;

(5) The scheme proposed by the expert meeting is more specific and comprehensive than that proposed by a member alone.

There are two forms of group brainstorming: direct brainstorming and questioning brainstorming.

The specific implementation of direct brainstorming can be divided into seven steps: (1) preparation; (2) warm-up; (3) introduction of problems; (4) renarration of problems; (5) selection of the most enlightening form of renarration; (6) putting forward various schemes through free talk; and (7) evaluating the schemes.

The Copywriting of Public Relations Planning

After designing the scheme, the public relations planners must write the contents of the scheme into a planning book, so as to get approval from the leaders and organize the implementation of the plan. The public relations planning book has something to do with copywriting.

The elements of the public relations planning copywriting consist of "5W" "2H" and "1E" as follows:

"5W"

(1) What—the purpose and contents of the plan;

(2) Who—the organizer, planner, and the public involved in the plan;

(3) Where—the place for the implementation of the plan;

(4) When—the opportunity for the implementation of the plan;

(5) Why—the reason for the plan;

"2H"

(1) How—methods and implementation forms of the plan;

(2) How much—budget of the plan.

"1E"

Effect—prediction of the results.

The basic format of a public relations planning book includes:

(1) Cover;

(2) Contents;

(3) Summary;

(4) Foreword;

(5) Environmental analysis;

(6) Establishment of objectives;

(7) Establishment of the public;

(8) Theme and publicity slogan of public relations activities;

(9) Implementation details;

(10) Necessary explanation.

Learning to Practice

Scan to Read More

In the autumn of 2020, Xiao Shaoyue left his hometown to Shaoxing by train from a small town in the north of Anhui Province, starting his "best youth" for four years.

He became a class monitor in his first year and president of the student union in his sophomore year. He took part in singing, running and debating competitions in his spare time. He studied hard, passed the extremely difficult national judicial examination, and obtained the Business English Translation Certificate. His four years of college life has seen a meaningful time.

He will start a business when he graduates. He chose a project and prepared a plan. What do you think are the main considerations in his plan?

Indication for Answer

Careful selection of entrepreneurial projects is the key to success. It is suggested that three points should be considered when writing the plan.

First, we must clearly know where the target customers are and understand their real needs. Second, we should start from small and fine, not big and comprehensive ones, and try our best to choose vertical fields for deep cultivation. Third, we should carefully design the profit mode, operation mode and management mode.

Case Study

Case 6.1 Chinese Netizens Urge Boycott of Marriott for Calling Tibet a "Country"

▶Replay of the Event

At 8:19 a.m. on January 9, 2018, a netizen named "Zhongjusaodi" posted that Marriott International sent a questionnaire survey via email to its elite members to collect feedback on its service and asked them to choose their country. The list included the "Chinese mainland" and "China's Tibet" separately.

The post was echoed by many netizens who claimed to be members of the company.[1]

---

[1] http://www.globaltimes.cn/content/1083995.shtml.

►Response

Marriott International has issued three statements on its Weibo account. Marriott Reward released a notice on its Weibo account on January 10, saying that "We are deeply sorry for the questionnaire. We realized that this mistake would deeply disappoint our Chinese customers. For now, we have suspended the questionnaire and will fix the options at once. We apologize for the inconvenience caused by the incident".

►Result

The netizen named Zhongjusaodi was the whistleblower, whose post has since been forwarded over 20,000 times and received more than 40,000 "likes". Many Chinese members of Marriott have said they will boycott its hotels, because such practice was totally unacceptable, hurting the feelings of Chinese people.

Authorities in Shanghai closed down Marriott International's Chinese website for a week, punishing the world's biggest hotel chain for listing Tibet as a country.[①] It also shut down Marriott's mobile phone application, a move that would disrupt bookings.

►Reflection

The hospitality giant sparked fury among Chinese netizens after it listed Tibet as a country in an email questionnaire to its members. Anger flared up after netizens found the same "mistake" on its smart phone application.[②] The storm caused by Marriott group has also affected other foreign-funded enterprises, including fast fashion giant Zara, Delta Airlines, Medtronic, etc., which have similar problems.

The planning is related to the future and for the future. Hence, while formulating plans, complete, clear and reliable knowledge should be collected and forecasts should be well prepared. The maximum results should be obtained from the minimum cost and effort when you make a plan.

---

① WANG Q C. Marriott in Hot Water for Misnaming Chinese Regions[EB/OL]. [2021-6-10]. https://www.shine.cn/news/nation/1801128958/.

② HUANG M. Marriott International under Investigation over Territorial Blunder[EB/OL]. [2021-6-10]. http://www.ecns.cn/2018/01-11/288027.shtml.

Case 6.2　JD.com Counterfeit Scandal

▶Replay of the Event

Just two days before Consumer Rights Day on March 15, 2018, a counterfeit scandal has become a nightmare for the JD company.

On March 13, Liu Liu, a renowned Chinese novelist published a post on her Weibo and WeChat accounts accusing JD Worldwide's store of selling a fake pillow product to her friend.[①]

Liu Liu said her friend ordered a Comfort U pillow from the United States, which is priced at about 1,489 yuan ($236) on JD Worldwide. But what her friend received was a Contour U pillow, which, according to the brand's official website, sells for just $34. Liu Liu and her friend concluded that JD Worldwide had attempted to charge full price for a cheap knockoff, and requested a full refund as well as a tenfold compensation as advertised on JD Worldwide. Online chat history posted by Liu Liu shows that the seller first denied that the product was different from what had been displayed on the site. After seeing evidence presented by the buyers, it agreed to give a refund but insisted that they had simply mailed the wrong product by mistake.

Liu Liu's Weibo post quickly gathered over 50,000 "likes" and 30,000 comments. On WeChat, it has been "liked" by more than 22,000 readers and viewed over 100,000 times.

▶Response

In response to the accusations, JD.com went on the offensive, issuing an official statement on March 14. It wrote that the customer had received the wrong product, not a fake. It also claimed that Liu Liu presented misleading information which seriously damaged the public image of the company, and that they would reserve the right to pursue legal action.

▶Result

The event caused a wider spread. On March 15, Liu Liu issued a Weibo post again to question JD, and said her WeChat official account was banned.

Finally, on March 17, JD CMO Xu Lei had to apologize and give a solution to

---

① PAN Y L. JD.com Counterfeit Scandal Kickstarts Consumer Rights Day in China[EB/OL]. [2021-6-15]. https://jingdaily.com/jd-counterfeit-scandal/.

improve the customer experience.

▶ Reflection

Although JD finally apologized for the incident, it was lucky to have made peace with the informant, and similar issues were not widely spread again. In September, JD fell into the abyss of public opinion due to the well-known events.

Case 6.3   Dolce & Gabbana Cancels Its Shanghai Great Show

▶ Replay of the Event

It was supposed to be the biggest fashion show in Dolce & Gabbana's 33-year history—a 300-plus-look, 140-performer, one-hour ode to China watched by a 1,400-strong audience crowded with local celebrities and influencers in Shanghai. On November 21, 2018, those plans collapsed into chaos as the company felt compelled to cancel the event after a controversy kindled by chopsticks escalated into a social media firestorm.[①] Three days ago, a short video was posted on Dolce & Gabbana's Instagram and Sina Weibo accounts, apparently intended to promote the upcoming Shanghai show. It released three trailers on social media to its show. The trailer series, titled "Eating with Chopsticks" consists of three episodes and is dubbed in Chinese with a young Asian-looking lady wearing D&G jewels and showing how to use a traditional wooden pair of chopsticks to eat Western foods.[②] In the trailers, the lady demonstrates how to use chopsticks to eat margherita pizza, Sicilian cannoli and Italian spaghetti, but the voiceovers ignited people's anger as the chopsticks are described as the little stick-shaped cutlery and pliers while the margherita pizza was described with the word "great" in one episode. The complaints about the content in the trailers have been continuously coming out in the comment sections of D&G posts, not only limited in the analogies since the series started being posted on Sunday. Some netizens also accused D&G of suggesting that Chinese people don't know how to eat Western foods. The ads have caused heated discussions on China's social media platforms.

---

① Dolce & Gabbana Cancels Its Shanghai Great Show amid Controversy[EB/OL]. [2021-6-16]. https:// www.vogue.com/article/dolce-gabbana-cancels-shanghai-great-show.

② GU L. Dolce & Gabbana Accused of Racism in Chinese Chopsticks Advertisements[EB/OL]. [2021-6-18]. http://www.ecns.cn/news/culture/2018-11-22/detail-ifzaaiuy4917792.shtml.

►Response

Screenshots filled with insulting comments on Chinese people by Dolce & Gabbana designer Stefano Gabbana were also seen spreading on social media, but Gabbana has denied the remarks in his account and said his account was hacked. But netizens questioned more drasticly on his explanation.

►Result

Chinese top celebrities including Zhang Ziyi, Li Bingbing, Chen Kun have confirmed their absence from Dolce & Gabbana's "The Great Show" fashion event.[①] On Chinese social media, the hashtags of "D&G Designer" and "D&G" immediately hit the ranks of hot searching with netizens starting to boycott the brand.

It's a pity for both sides. Mistakes have been made by Dolce & Gabbana, and when the problem blew up on social media, they didn't act fast enough to explain themselves, and it became news across the world.

At noon on November 23, D&G officials finally released an apology video in which the company's founder said "I'm sorry" in Chinese. However, this has come after a fact that China's online sales channels and offline stores had shown approval to close the door to D&G.

►Reflection

There are many aspects in D&G's public relations mistakes that we should pay attention to. One is that there is no standard and restriction on the speech and behavior of the company leaders, but it doesn't mean that they can speak arbitrarily without planning, regardless of the corporate image and interests. The second is that deceiving the masses with such a lame lie as "account being hacked" can obtain no trust at all. If the enterprise really has encountered technological problems, it is necessary to admit that it cannot shirk its responsibility and plan for the next scheme. Moreover, it should correct itself in the management of the enterprise. In fact, finding and solving the problem is a great opportunity to grow for the enterprise. Never let users lose confidence in the enterprise.

Courseware   Quiz

① LI Y. Italian Fashion Brand D&G Ads Spark Fury in China[EB/OL]. [2021-6-20]. http://www.ecns.cn/news/society/2018-11-21/detail-ifzaaiuy4917363.shtml.

Chapter 7

Publicity—the Original Idea of Public Relations Communication

Preparation for Start

Scan to Dialogue   Scan to Listen

Information is the stuff of communication. If you were a salesman, you sell at your best-selling point. Requirements for public relations personnel are similar. They need to be aware of their special abilities and advantages. For example, Zhang Shan has extensive and amazing people skills, and this quality has been proven at work. His co-workers have often complimented him that he makes the work place energetic and positive with his people skills.

Understanding Objectives

PUBLIC RELATIONS

After studying Chapter 7, you should be able to:

1. Understand the theories of public relations communication.

2. List main media that public relations personnel often choose to facilitate communication.

3. Master the main principles of media choice for public relations communication.

Basic Concepts and Elements

PUBLIC RELATIONS

Communication is a social behavior of human beings to exchange information, a process in which information, perceptions and ideas are transferred and shared among people. "All of the incidents exist for the purpose of conveying, sharing, or processing information in some way."[①] Public relations communication refers to the process that organizations use various media to communicate with the public and strive for understanding and trust.

When a practitioner attempts to make a product newsworthy in order to get attention from media and the public, it is called product publicity. Publicity is the process when

---

① 施拉姆,波特.传播学概论[M].北京:北京大学出版社,2007:36.

information is provided by PR practitioners for the media to use because the information has news value. It is an uncontrolled method of placing messages in the media because the source does not pay for placement. The practitioners can control advertising, but not publicity, which is the major difference between publicity and advertising. When an organization communicates to its publics, publicity is one of the tactics. Publicity is the naivety of public relations communication strategies.

Characteristics of Public Relations Communication

Public relations communication is different from the general news communication, and also different from the general propaganda and advertisement. It can be classified as subordinate communication, two-way communication and intermediary communication.

1. Subordinate Communication

This is similar to advertising, but different from news and publicity. In some countries, news media is the mouthpiece of the government or party. It is a fundamental task to correctly publicize the goverment's or the party's lines, principles and policies. Other organizations are different. The dissemination of organizational information must be based on its target objectives from the perspective of organizational levels, using different ways to seek the development of the organization.

2. Two-Way Communication

The public relations communication requires a two-way form in purpose, basis, means, and procedures.

In terms of purpose, to create a good image in the eyes of the public, it is necessary to first understand what the public wants.

In terms of basis, the organization's objectives, the interest relations, the decision-making process, the content of communication and the scheme should be determined according to the interests of both the organization and the public.

In terms of means and procedures, the public relations practice is always a two-way communication process, that is, from the organization to the public, and then from the public back to the organization. Through the dissemination of information, an organization tells the public its goals, policies and specific measures, so that the public can understand the organization; the public tells the organization its requirements, opinions and suggestions through investigation or active communication and complaints, so that the organization can understand the public. Through this two-way communication, mutual understanding and trust can be established, thus enhancing the relationship between the two sides.

3. Intermediary Communication

As public relations communication is a two-way communication, it only serves as a bridge between the organization and the public. It is neither an end nor a subject, but a tool. The subject of journalism and communication is media, especially the rules of media. Understanding media means understanding communication. If we master the law of media, we will master the law of communication. This is the difference between public relations communication and other forms of communication.

Communication Theories Related to Public Relations

Theories can provide an understanding of the relationship between actions and events if you need to explain why and how your plans and proposals will work. However, there is no one theory that can explain all public relations communication.

The process of communication includes six elements, namely: subject, content, media, object, effect and feedback. The analysis of these six elements constitutes the main contents of modern communication science.

(1) Control analysis: To study the subject of communication (i. e., the question of "who"), which is the source and producer of information.

(2) Content analysis: To study the content of communication (i. e., the question of "what is said"), which is the way of making information content.

(3) Media analysis: To study the media of communication (i.e., the question of "what channel to pass"), which includes the types, functions and characteristics of media.

(4) Audience analysis: To study the object of communication (i.e., the question of "to whom"), namely, the classification of the public.

(5) Effect analysis: To study the effect of communication (i.e., the degree of change in the opinion, attitude and behavior of the communication subject to the public).

(6) Feedback analysis: To study the feedback from communicators, including the constraints that objects have on subjects.

Several communication theories related to public relations will be introduced as follows.

►Agenda Setting Theory

Setting the agenda describes the mass media's significant, and sometimes controversial role in determining which topics are at the center of public attention and action. Although Walter Lippmann captured the essence of the media's powerful influence early in the 20th century with his phrase, "the world outside and the pictures in our heads", a detailed, empirical elaboration of this agenda setting role of the mass media did not begin until the final quarter of the 20th century. Maxwell McCombs, one of the founding fathers of agenda setting tradition of research, synthesizes hundreds of scientific studies carried out on this central role of the mass media in the shaping of public opinion. Across the world, the mass media strongly influences what the pictures of public affairs in our heads are about. The mass media also influences the very details of those pictures. In addition to describing this media influence on what we think about and how we think about it, setting the agenda also discusses the sources of these media agendas, the psychological explanation for their impact on the public agenda, and the subsequent consequences for attitudes, opinions and behaviors.

Media influence affects the presenting order of events and issues in a news report to the public mind. More importance there is to a piece of news, more importance is attributed by audience (Media Priorities). These are the levels of Agenda Setting Theory:

First level: Mostly studied by researchers, the media uses objects or issues to influence what people think about.

Second level: The media focuses on how people think.

Agenda Setting Theory has been used in political advertising, campaigns, business news, public relations, etc. The main concept associated with the theory is gatekeeping. Gatekeeping controls over the selection of content discussed in the media; the public cares mostly about the product of media gatekeeping. The media editors themselves are especially gatekeepers. News media decides "what" events to transmit through the "gates" on ground of "news worthiness". For example, when news comes from various sources, the editors choose what should appear and what should not. That's why they are called "gatekeepers". Primary activity of the media in proposing the values and standards can be judged. The contents showing up in media will usually be more vivid than the actual situations. To say it in simple words, when the media gives utmost importance to a piece of news, it leaves people the impression that the news contains the most important information. Headlines, special news features, discussions, expert opinions are used to achieve this effect.

▶ Balance Theory

Several related theories focus on the consistency of information and how people process messages. Balance Theory, articulated by psychologist Fritz Heider, observes that unbalanced mental stances create tension and force an individual to try to restore the balance. Balance Theory states that the market will tend toward equilibrium. Fritz Heider proposed that people will attempt to maintain a psychological balance and form relationships that balance out their likes and dislikes. For example, if Person A likes a celebrity and the celebrity likes a product, but Person A originally disliked the product, then Person A is likely to end up increasing his enjoyment of the product or decreasing his liking of the celebrity or both. All these options create equilibrium.[1]

Charles Osgood and Percy Tannenbaum's Congruity Theory added some measurement in attitude. The lesson of these consistency theories for public relations practitioners is that attitude change can be stimulated by information that causes people to realize that two attitudes are in conflict.

►Cultivation Theory

In the late 1960s, the social influence of television media, especially the negative effect, was growing. The problem of violence and crime in the United States was very serious. George Gerbner studied the influence of watching TV on people's ideas, attitudes and values from two aspect. The first is to analyze the relationship between murder and violence in TV pictures and social crimes; the second is to investigate the influence of these contents on people's understanding of social reality.

Cultivation Theory, proposed by George Gerbner, suggests that the media (notably television) shapes or cultivates peoples' conception of social reality. A large amount of media exposure over time affects not only individuals but also society as a whole. Gerbner argued that television cultivated a middle-of-the-road political perspective, though more recent observers have noted that, with the fragmentation of media and the 24/7 news cycle on politics-oriented TV networks, the effect now is more divisive in society. Gerbner also articulated the mean world effect. This effect observes that people who use the media a lot tend to be more fearful, suspicious of the world, and susceptible to social paranoia and conspiracy theories.

►Innovation Diffusion Theory

The Innovation Diffusion Theory works when all kinds of people's adoption of innovation are studied and classified. Its theoretical ideology is that in front of innovation, some people will be more open-minded than others and are willing to adopt creativity. Everett Rogers studied how innovations are spread (or diffused) throughout the society, shedding light on the likelihood that new ideas or products will be adopted. He identified five categories of adopters (innovators, early adopters, early majority, late majority and laggards). The theory provides insight for public relations practitioners on who and how to address messages

---

[1] http://www.investorwords.com/15193/balance_theory.html.

about new concepts.

▶ Sleeper Effect

Researchers have observed that sometimes the persuasive impact of communication increases as time elapses. Carl Hovland and Walter Weiss identified this Sleeper Effect.

Because of the time interval, it is easy for people to forget the source of information, and only retain a vague memory of the content. In attitudinal psychology, people call the phenomenon where the influence of the speaker's prestige has the opposite effect with the passage of time the "sleeper effect".

In short, what people may have initially received from a source with low credibility can eventually become separated from the source, leading to an increase in message credibility. Conversely, what people initially considered a highly persuasive message may fade over time.

▶ Framing Theory

Framing is a process of selective control. There are two meanings:

(1) The way in which news content is typically shaped and contextualized within the same frame of reference;

(2) The audience adopts the frame of reference and sees the world in a similar way. It is about how people attach importance to news and perceive its context within which an issue is viewed.

Whereas agenda setting deals with the perceived news worthiness of an issue, framing focuses on the presentation of the message—how the media not only focus on a topic but, more significantly, how they present the topic to their audience. Framing Theory, first articulated by Gregory Bateson, thus provides a rhetorical context for the message. Seen often in coverage of political news or social issues, Framing Theory attempts to explain how the news media frame a story. Is a political candidate "ahead" "surging" or "falling behind"? Is there an inherent "good guy" or "bad guy" in the story? Whose version of events gets top billing? Which version becomes the standard against which other points of view are measuring? Public relations practitioners also use framing, especially in communication vehicles that are aimed at their publics without needing the involvement of the news media, such as through direct mails, websites, blogs, brochures and social media.

▶ Gatekeeper Theory

Kurt Lewin, a German-born American social psychologist known for his field theory of behavior, holds that human behavior is a function of an individual's psychological environment. The concept of gatekeeping originated from his work about a post-World War II study on how families select foods. Lewin compared decision-making filters to gates because entry can either be permitted or denied by the gatekeeper. Lewin proposed that the process of filtering, selecting and rejecting objects, according to a set of criteria, was relevant to the news selection process.

Lewin's study inspired the future work of David Manning White, a journalism and communication scholar, who researched how American newsrooms practiced gatekeeping in 1949. White learned that news organizations filter news through multiple "gates" before the daily news is selected. He found that reporters and editors acted as gatekeepers who shaped the nature of the stories by determining whether the story should be publicized and if so, what aspects should be emphasized for the public.[1] Anyone who decides whether information should be shared with the public can be classified as a gatekeeper.[2]

► Two-Step Flow Theory

The two-step flow model hypothesizes that ideas flow from mass media to opinion leaders, and from them to a wider population. It was first introduced by sociologist Paul Lazarsfeld et al. in 1944[3] and elaborated by Elihu Katz and Lazarsfeld in 1955[4] and subsequent publications. Communication is a complex and complicated art that is made up of rich theories and hypotheses. These theories attempt to explain the usefulness and importance of mass media, advertising, public relations and more. One theory that has always been popular and thoroughly talked about in research and academic studies is the Two-Step Flow Theory. The theory explains how information from the media moves in two distinct stages. The hypothesis states that ideas often flow from radios and prints to opinion leaders and from them to the less active sections of the population. The Two-Step Flow Theory furthers the understanding of how mass media influence decision-making by refining the ability to predict how messages will have an effect on audiences and why certain campaigns succeed in changing audience opinions. These actions are done through influential opinion

① https://gatekeepinginonlinejournalism.fandom.com/wiki/The_Origin_of_Gatekeeping_Theory.

② DIMITROVA D, CONNOLLY-AHERN C. Hyperlinking as Gatekeeping: Online Newspaper Coverage of the Execution of an American Terrorist[J]. Journalism Studies, 2003, 4(3): 401-414.

③ LAZARSFELD P, BERELSON B, GAUDET H. The People's Choice: How the Voter Makes up His Mind in a Presidential Campaign[M]. New York: Columbia University Press, 1944: 151.

④ KATZ E, LAZARSFELD P, ROSHWALB I. Personal Influence: The Part Played by People in the Flow of Mass Communications[J]. Journal of Marketing, 1955, 21(1): 309.

leaders and their effects on the thought processes of their audiences.

The Two-Step Flow Theory works as follows: An intermediary is introduced between the sender, or the mass media, and the audience. This new or secondary step in the dissemination of information is typically conducted by an influential figure or opinion leader with greater access to information than the audience. They have the authority to dissect and explain the message as they please and, subsequently, influence the opinions of the final receivers, or the individuals in social contact with them. Opinion leaders, also known as public opinion directors, refer to those who have more opportunities to receive information from various channels in social activities, or have rich knowledge and experience in a certain field, that is, authoritative experts. Their attitudes and opinions have a greater impact on the general public.

One of the most important parts of this theory that directly affects the movement of the message and its impact is the beliefs and ideas of the personal contact or opinion leader. The information coming from the opinion leader is altered with personal opinions and research, thus the original message is not the same as it started in the media. Opinion leaders are much more exposed to mass media and much more engaged in active communication than the general public is and are not passive gatekeepers of media information. If they did not transmit the contents based on their own opinions, then there would be no communication hypothesis challenging the strong media effects.

Another important part of the Two-Step Flow Theory to understand is that audiences are more likely to be influenced by others like themselves, which alters where and how they are receiving the information. Opinion leaders are almost equal in proportions in every social group and stratum and there is a homogeneity of opinions amongst these groups. For an audience, opinion leaders and their personal influences are trustworthy, flexible and non-purposive because they are similar. For example, religious persons are more likely to listen to their pastor because he or she is equal to their status and shares many of the same beliefs.

This theory is important to public relations professionals because they must take opinion leaders into consideration while creating campaigns. They must also work with the opinion leaders and rely on them to help bypass the media. Audiences and opinion leaders are two of the most important parts of public relations and the Two-Step Flow Theory affects them in a way that cannot be ignored.[1]

---

[1] https://sites.psu.edu/tizio/two-step-flow-theory/.

Media of Public Relations Communication

Media, in the sense of communication, refers to the intermediary through which the process of communication can be realized, and it is a physical form that carries, replicates and transmits information. The communication media has experienced four stages: (1) oral media stage; (2) hand-copied media stage; (3) printing media stage; (4) electronic media stage.

The advantages of oral media are: (1) no auxiliary means are needed, easy to use and control; (2) two-way communication to achieve "targeted"; (3) it can release people's emotional energy and play a certain role in psychological balance. The disadvantages are: (1) the transmission distance is short and the coverage is narrow; (2) the oral language disappears quickly and is difficult to be directly preserved; (3) the oral information is easy to be distorted.

The advantages of hand-copied media are: (1) the transmission distance is extended and the range is large; (2) the information can be saved and will not disappear rapidly; (3) the information transmission has exact reliability. The disadvantages are: (1) slow transmission speed, small information capacity, small scale and high cost; (2) limitations of text information transmission.

The advantages of printing media are: (1) it can copy and transmit information on a large scale, which greatly reduces the communication cost and speeds up the transmission; (2) the scope of communication is not the same as that of other media, and its information capacity is also increasing; (3) it has unique conditions for information preservation. The disadvantages are: (1) the transmission channel is single; (2) the selectivity is limited.

The advantages of electronic media are: (1) the transmission speed is faster, the scope is wider, and it has various transmission channels, which can meet different requirements of the receiver; (2) it can often be synchronized with emergency events, so that the receiver has a sense of being in the scene, and its appeal and acceptability are greatly increased; (3) benefiting from sounds and pictures, receivers of different cultural levels can obtain reliable information that can be understood or needed. The disadvantages are: (1) poor direct recording; (2) insufficient selectivity.

Newspapers are cheaper, easy to store and have a wide range of reading choices. The information obtained is professional and authoritative. However, newspapers have requirements for reading ability, and the information updating is not as timely as the network and other new media.

Articles in magazines have strong pertinence, and the period of information coverage and updating is long; many magazines are well printed, beautifully bound and have high preservation value. However, magazines have several shortcomings: (1) lack of flexibility and timeliness; (2) limited reading range; (3) poor attraction.

Broadcasting is a means of mass communication in which the sound is transmitted by radio waves or wires. Advantages: (1) fast and timely, strong timeliness; (2) ultra far coverage, strong permeability; (3) strong voice, emotion and appeal; (4) both refined and popular with a strong mass character. Disadvantages: (1) fleeting; (2) sequential listening with poor selectivity; (3) poor image sense.

Television is a mass media tool with sound and image transmitted through radio waves. Television combines the art of sound and vision; it holds strong sense of scene and high credibility. However, TV interviews may just show the surface of the informations, and the reflection cannot be the reproduced. Also, the high cost prevents people from using TV talk shows to communicate.

The Internet refers to the largest, open and interconnected network in the world, which mainly adopts TCP/IP protocols. The Internet began in 1969. It is compatible, interactive, global and immediate with strong pertinence. The information on the Internet can be easily stored and retrieved. However, the information on the Internet can be fake because it lacks preciseness, authority, and rules. Sometimes it also lacks depth and originality.

Some communication is non-verbal. Keith Coleman divided non-verbal communication into three categories: (1) marker language; (2) action language; (3) object language.

The characteristics of non-verbal communication are: (1) communicable; (2) situational; (3) credible; (4) combinatorial; (5) metaphorical. On the one hand, non-verbal communication has a supplementary function to verbal communication; on the other hand, non-verbal symbols can add some annotations to verbal communication.

The Choice of Media and Media Combination

The most commonly used communication channels of public relations are interpersonal communication channels, organizational communication channels and mass communication channels.

It is the media that supports people's communication in various channels. The principles of selecting media for PR practitioners include: (1) the characteristics of the target audience; (2) the characteristics of the media and its influence on the target audience; (3) the characteristics of the information; (4) the selection and the media utilization of the competitors; (5) the organization's economic benefits.

We need to conduct in-depth analysis according to the characteristics of the target audience, and then choose different media to release information. First of all, we should select the media according to the actual situation of the target audience; the second factor is the contact rate of media and the third one is the habits of the target audience. Of course, in the specific implementation of public relations communication program, we should also consider the following factors—the natural conditions, climate conditions and average living standards of the target audience's residential area, and so on.

Evaluating the influence of a medium can not only examine its quality, for example, the quality of a magazine's print, but also the amount, such as the volume of page viewing in a WeChat official account.

We can combine a variety of media for public relations communication. Media combination can also be called media integration. The basic consideration of media combination is to rationally allocate and utilize the media resources with limited funds from a global perspective to achieve the best effect of information dissemination.

Media combination should meet the following six requirements: (1) the serialization and clearance of the organization's information in terms of content and form of expression; (2) establishment of a good image for product or service; (3) access to and influence on the target audience; (4) the effective implementation or countermeasures to the information dissemination by competitors; (5) the accurate timing of information dissemination; (6) the diversity of media.

There are many advantages of media combination: (1) it can produce the multi-level information; (2) it can make the information spread intensively; (3) it can bring the best effect caused by the impact; (4) it can achieve the maximum arrival rate.

There are two ways of media combination:

(1) Centralized media combination, which is to put limited advertising expenses into a specific medium. This kind of combination can exert the maximum impact on the target objects identified by the organization, and then form a strong intimacy of these audiences to the products or services. The centralized media combination is suitable for a specific and known range of audiences who have formed certain media contact habits.

(2) Decentralized media combination, which is to organize and use different media to transmit relevant information to different groups of people.

Learning to **P**ractice

Scan to Read More

At present, the enforcement scope of the comprehensive administrative law of urban management includes: city appearance and environmental sanitation, urban planning management, road traffic order, industrial and commercial administration, municipal administration, public utility management, urban water-saving management, parking management, garden greening management, environmental protection management, construction site management, urban river and lake management, and so on. Urban management personnel can punish construction without license, illegal occupation of roads, and operations alike. On August 14, 2020, a video went viral on the Internet. As can be seen from the video, four urban management personnel held and pushed over an old lady selling vegetables several times. Although there were many people around dissuading the action, they didn't stop. If you were the public relations director of the local urban management department, how would you respond to the public?

Indication for **A**nswer

Obviously, you can't allow all the media to enter the management department. Even if you have good relationships with the media reporters, it's impossible to answer their questions through several phone calls. You're very passive, and you'll soon find that you don't have enough time. You can set up an information center to deal with rumors and handle requests for information from the public and mass media. Of course, the task of answering all public questions cannot be entrusted to the center. You also need to establish a coordinating center through which all information between your department and the press could flow.

Specifically speaking, you can first respond as follows: In the process of maintaining business order in the street, the staff of the management department had different opinions with the mobile vendors, which caused physical conflicts. The relevant staff members have been suspended, and the public security organs have set about an investigation, so as to rightly deal with the relevant people according to law and discipline based on the investigation results.

Case Study

PUBLIC RELATIONS

BGI and Media

The relationship between an enterprise and the media can be studied from different angles. For example, from the perspective of ownership, we can examine whether a medium belongs to the enterprise itself or is an external one. BGI (Beijing Genomics Institute) has its own media system, such as website, Sino Weibo, and WeChat official account. After 2017, the information of the BGI stock has been released through its own media accounts. As a leading science and technology enterprise, BGI also had news releases in newspapers, radio and television before. Being a leader in the industry, BGI enjoys the reputation of "Tencent in gene sequencing", and has several large bioinformatics supercomputing centers in Shenzhen, Hong Kong, Beijing, Wuhan and Hangzhou. It has obvious advantages in technology, qualification and genome database in China. After the listing in 2017, various news about BGI has appeared in the new media. According to the reports, Wang Jian, chairman of the board, is not used to dealing with media and other public relations activities. He was said to twice refuse to ring the bell himself.

At the launch ceremony, BGI gave the opportunity to six special people, including a representative of "Tang Baobao" (baby with Down's syndrome), a representative who had benefitted from BGI testing, and a representative caring for rare diseases and the disabled groups. The reporter of *China Securities Journal* observed that in fact, Wang Jian refused two important opportunities to ring the bell: The first was to ring the bell for listing, and the second was to ring the bell for the company's directors and executives. After ringing the bell for listing, the Shenzhen Stock Exchange lowered the bell as usual for the participants to take photos. At this stage, a group of directors and senior executives of BGI stepped on stage to ring the bell to commemorate the event. However, Wang Jian stepped down and quit from the photo area.[①]

BGI shares performed well after its listing. On November 14, 2017, the highest stock price of BGI was 261.99 yuan, and the closing price of that day was 255.88 yuan, an

---

① http://finance. sina. com. cn/stock/s/2017-07-14/doc-ifyiakwa4154717. shtml? cre=financepagepc&mod=f& loc=4&r=9&doct=0&rfunc=100.

increase of 4.86%. Since then, the stock price has increased more than 17 times, and the market value of the company rapidly exceeded 100 billion yuan in just four months, ranking the top three of the A-share pharmaceutical listed companies.

From the source of media content, we can tell whether an enterprise provides the information for the media itself, or the media obtains the information from other channels. For example, in the statement on July 13, 2018, BGI specially reminded the investors that the exclusive media designated by the company were *China Securities Journal*, *Securities Times*, *Shanghai Securities News*, and *Securities Daily*. All the disclosed information shall be subject to the announcement published in the above designated media. Since then, the statement has repeatedly stressed that these media were the exclusive ones.

This is in accordance with Article 6 of the Measures for the Administration of Information Disclosure of Listed Companies: When listed companies and other obligors disclose information according to the law, they shall submit the draft of the announcement and relevant documents to the stock exchange for registration, and publish them in the media designated by the China Securities Regulatory Commission (hereinafter referred to as the CSRC). The four newspapers mentioned above, as well as *Securities Market Weekly*, are professional newspapers designated by the CSRC.

In the Internet era, many media just provide a platform, and the information contents are generated and provided by the users and published on their own accounts. Social media has made users more widely distributed and become a large source of information.

From the nature of media content, we can tell whether it is beneficial or unfavorable to the relevant enterprises. The benefitial content plays a positive role in the reputation and development of the enterprise; the unfavorable content has a negative effect on the development of the enterprise and will damage its reputation. In 2018, BGI encountered several major public relations crises, one of which had a fairly satisfactory ending, while some others went to the court for verdicts.

Case 7.1 Enclose Incident on Tianya Forum

► Replay of the Event

Wang Deming, head of Nanjing Changjianyujia Company and a former partner of BGI, said that on January 16, 2018, he received an express mail from BGI, which stated that BGI wanted to cancel the cooperation with his company. Since then, he and BGI have had five months of communication, and the two sides failed to reach an agreement. This pushed Nanjing Changjianyujia Company to the critical point of survival.

Paradoxically, according to numerous media reports in Nanjing, on May 20, 2018, Nanjing Municipal Government and Jiangbei New District signed a strategic cooperation framework agreement with BGI respectively to jointly build health care big data center and gene technology R&D and application demonstration base. The government officials and Wang Jian, the chairman of BGI, attended the event and witnessed the signing of contract.[1]

But a few days later, on May 29, 2018, BGI published a statement claiming that Nanjing Changjianyujia Health Management Co., Ltd. pretended to be "Jiangsu Operation Center of the National Gene Bank" in *Jiangsu Financial Report*, refuting its existence, and declared that it had terminated the cooperative relations with Changjianyujia. According to the statement, BGI has never authorized Changjianyujia to carry out market activities and make relevant remarks in the name of "Jiangsu Operation Center of the National Gene Bank", and has never designated Wang Deming, an employee of the company, as the director of the above-mentioned organization.

On June 14, 2018, Wang Deming published an article on Tianya Forum in the name of "Dugu Jiujian Wang Deming", reporting BGI's high-tech fraud, suspected bribery, and large-scale state-owned assets defraud.

▶ Response

In June 27, 2018, BGI issued a solemn statement through its official account in response to Wang Deming's accusation. It stated that: (1) It has terminated all the cooperative relations with Nanjing Changjianyujia; (2) There is no organization named "Jiangsu Operation Center of the National Gene Bank"; (3) BGI did not participate in any real estate projects in Jiangsu Province and did not obtain land resources. At the same time, the reason why BGI had terminated the contract with Changjianyujia was that the latter failed to meet the assessment criteria. According to the technical service contract signed by both parties, the target of sample tasks of Changjianyujia in 2017 was 300 cases, but merely 17 cases were actually completed, with the completion rate of only 5.7%.[2]

Wang Deming, on the other hand, said that BGI IPO in 2017 did not include cell business in the materials it submitted to the CSRC. In order to avoid the impact of cell business on the listing, all the operation centers were stopped for the time being, so the completion rate was not high. Wang Deming stressed that the 5.7% performance ranked second among 11 agents nationwide, second only to the Guangdong agent, where the

---

[1] http://jsnews.jschina.com.cn/nj/a/201805/t20180522_1620072.shtml.

[2] https://mp.weixin.qq.com/s/4H8Xz84jmSGTBq0XjcXUag.

headquarters of BGI was based. He believes that the real cause of BGI's termination of the contract is that stem cell therapy and biological therapy may become a trend in the future, with a broad market prospect. And BGI hopes to monopolize this business and outsource its agency to companies which have a closer relationship with itself.

Wang Deming released some messages again in his WeChat account on September 14, 2018, claiming that he would "commit suicide" at headquarters of the National Gene Bank on September 22.

On September 15, 2018, BGI released an article "Cherish Life and Respect the Law" through its WeChat official account, saying it sincerely hoped and implored Wang Deming to cherish his life and did not want any tragedy or extreme event to happen.

On the evening of September 16, 2018, Wang Deming once again published an article and said that the cloud disk containing relevant evidence of BGI would be released before his suicide on September 22, and he would carry a USB flash disk on his body for the use of the police. The U-disk will contain all the truth as well as his last words.

At the same time, BGI also sent an executive to Wang Deming's hometown in Shandong to meet Wang's friends at the weekend, hoping to dissuade Wang. On the evening of September 17, Wang's lawyer talked with the executive for nearly an hour to discuss the matter.

Later, it was reported that BGI was willing to pay Wang Deming 15 million yuan in cash. On the afternoon of September 19, Zhu Yanmei, the executive vice president of BGI, who could not contact Wang Deming through various channels, publicly told Wang Deming, "As long as you promise not to hurt yourself and other people, and your demands are reasonable and legal, I am willing to meet you anywhere and sit down to talk. I am also willing to pay your counsel fees." Five minutes later, Wang Deming tweeted that he would not commit suicide.

On the afternoon of September 20, three senior executives of BGI, including Zhu Yanmei, and a lawyer came to Nanchang to have a face-to-face communication with Wang Deming and his lawyer. Wang Deming once again promised that he would not do anything stupid.[1]

After the "report gate" fermented, Changjianyujia and BGI launched a seesaw battle for several months. Both sides insisted on their own opinions and sued each other for infringement of reputation rights on relevant matters.

---

[1] https://zhuanlan.zhihu.com/p/94735000.

►Result

On the afternoon of March 15, 2019, People's Court in Yantian District Shenzhen made the first instance judgment on the case of BGI suing Wang Deming for reputation infringement. According to the judgment, the court held that the contents released by the defendant Wang Deming on the Internet objectively decreased the social preference of the plaintiff, BGI, which constituted reputation infringement. Therefore, within 10 days of the judgment, Wang Deming must issue a statement for three consecutive days through Tianya Forum to publicly apologize to the plaintiff and eliminate the impact.[1]

►Reflection

Tianya community is known as the "global online Chinese home". Since its establishment on March 1, 1999, it has been highly praised by Internet users at home and abroad for its openness, inclusiveness and humanistic care. After more than ten years of development, it has become a comprehensive virtual community and large-scale social network platform based on forum, blog and microblog, which provides a series of functional services such as personal space, enterprise space, shopping street, wireless client, classified information, and Q&A. Tianya community covers more than 200 million quality users and 85 million registered users every month. It is a leading platform of network events and celebrities for Chinese people.

After the listing of BGI, the performance at the beginning period was good and promising. The company's top managers adjusted its future development strategy, resulting in the termination of contracts with 11 enterprises that it had previously cooperated. These were all reasonable commercial activities within the scope of the law. However, there would be many difficulties in the specific implementation process. Pacifying the parties concerned and cooperating with the media is an important issue to consider. Especially for people like Wang Deming, who has both media experience and media resources, as well as some complex personal problems. It is necessary to do a good PR job patiently and carefully, so as to avoid major negative news in the media and adverse public opinions, which will directly affect the reputation of the enterprise and its stock price.

---

[1] https://tech.sina.com.cn/d/i/2019-03-15/doc-ihrfqzkc4198536.shtml.

Case 7.2 "Gene Detection Gate" of Huxiu Website

►Replay of the Event

On July 13, 2018, Botong, a user of the Huxiu website, released a report entitled "BGI Cancer". Some doubts were disclosed about the non-invasive prenatal gene testing technology and related business of the company in China. A family in Hunan Province was misdiagnosed by three doctors in a row and ignored or abandoned four other tests, the report said. It is this series of misdiagnoses and neglects that led to the complete failure of the production inspection. The root cause was the "non-invasive low-risk" report by BGI. It also said that the "harm reduction and coke reduction" scheme by BGI was a fraud and that BGI was an accomplice of China's tobacco system.

►Response

On July 13, 2018, BGI released an announcement on it's official WeChat account in response to the report on Huxiu website. BGI denied that there was exaggeration about the effect of non-invasive prenatal gene testing. It also stressed the significance of providing basic research services for CNTC and its subsidiaries.[1]

On July 15, 2018, BGI released another "letter to pregnant mothers" on its official website and WeChat account. According to the Guidelines on Pre-pregnancy and Pregnancy Health Care (2018 Edition) issued by the Chinese Medical Association, the letter said, each pregnant mother will undergo 7 to 11 different prenatal examinations, and the non-invasive prenatal genetic testing was only one of them; the case of accident was not caused by the company's non-invasive prenatal genetic testing.

►Result

With the decline of people's attention, the whole incident has also gradually ceased.

"People's Voice" column of the Rednet is a special zone for Hunan netizens to reflect their life problems. On April 21, 2018, a netizen reported that during her pregnancy, she had a prenatal examination in Wangcheng Maternal and Child Health Hospital, including more than ten routine examinations, three B-ultrasound examinations and one non-invasive DNA examination, which cost nearly 10,000 yuan. However, due to the carelessness and irresponsibility of doctors in the hospital, her child was born improperly with multiple

---

[1] https://mp.weixin.qq.com/s/gYavZXwjO4JtdDAQmlyL_w.

disabilities. However, she found that during the period from February to September 2017, the hospital was not qualified for obstetric examination. So she asked Wangcheng District Health and Family Planning Bureau and higher authorities to intervene in the investigation. The bureau mentioned in its reply that it had organized the netizen, the hospital and BGI to mediate for many times, but no consensus was reached. Therefore, it was suggested that the netizen should protect her rights through judicial appraisal. This indicates that BGI has already had experience in dealing with similar events before Huxiu reflected the problem. Although netizens did not directly point the spearhead at BGI, the relevant public relations personnel of BGI should have a plan.

►Reflection

Founded in May 2012, the Huxiu website is a new media platform integrating high-quality innovative information and people, aiming to provide more efficient communicating experiences for business users. This platform focuses on the contribution of original, in-depth, sharp and high-quality business information, where the netizens can analyze and exchange views on innovation and entrepreneurship. The platform has gathered more than 2,000 high-quality business editors, authors and third-party media. It seems that there is no difficulty for BGI to deal with the complaints posted on Huxiu. Probably it was not completely CBI's fault? Or it was just because some medical institutions and personnel have overstated the effect of non-invasive gene testing, which finally led to blind obedience and even irresponsibility. Although this post has been forwarded by many websites, there was little doubt about BGI. This event, however, superimposed with the previous events, had an immeasurable impact on China's gene project industry.

Under normal circumstances, it is unacceptable for the public to witness a tragedy in an industry, while the leading enterprises are indifferent to it. In response, BGI neither considered itself responsible nor proposed improvement measures. However, from the perspective of public relations communication, even if BGI was not responsible for this incident, in terms of the influence on the public attitude, BGI still needs to take some measures to fulfill the public's expectations and show its sincere attitudes.

Courseware   Quiz

Chapter 8
Practice of Public Relations Special Activities

Preparation for **S**tart

Scan to Dialogue   Scan to Listen

Everyone entering an industry will have their own career planning. What do you hope to do with your career? I love television and entertainment, so I would love to begin my career in media industry. My ultimate dream is to be a successful media mogul. My friend's ideal is to be a CEO one day; therefore, he has tried his best to learn the knowledge of running a company. Let's improve ourselves in the practice of public relations and gradually realize our professional ideals.

Understanding **O**bjectives

After studying Chapter 8, you should be able to:

1. Understand the theories of public relations special activities.

2. List main public relations special activities.

3. Prepare before a press conference for public relations.

4. Master some crisis-management skills.

Basic **C**oncepts and **E**lements

Special activities, also known as special events or programs, are one of the contents of PR work in enterprises. Organizations or enterprises, in order to achieve their goals in public relations, apart from the daily activities, will invite the press and the public to participate in some special activities and make full use of various media.

Daily Public Relations Activities

According to the business types, daily public relations activities can be divided into:

(1) Publicity. It mainly includes printing media, electronic media and other propaganda

means to transmit the organization's information, influence the public opinion, and rapidly expand the social impact of the organization.

(2) Social interaction. It mainly includes various communication methods and arts, such as making friends, coordinating relations, easing and resolving conflicts, and creating a harmonious social environment for the organization.

Social interaction is the most widely used mode of public relations because of its outstanding effect in strengthening emotional contact.

(3) Service-oriented activity. It is a public relations mode in which organizations provide various beneficial services to the public. It shows the purpose, nature and sincerity of the organization by means of attracting the public, influencing people, winning praise, striving for cooperation, making the relationship between the organization and the public more harmonious, and improving the social reputation of the organization.

Service-oriented activity is the most easily accepted form to the public.

(4) Social benefit activity. It mainly functions in the name of the organization, and acts as the leading role or enthusiastic participant in social development.

The characteristics of social benefit activity lie in its services for the public welfare and its cultural nature. It can be an important activity of an organization, a cultural event, a social welfare undertaking, or a news unit consisting of a variety of activities jointly organized by some enterprises.

(5) Consultation. This type of activity is mainly based on information collection, public opinion survey and poll. It provides the basis for organizational decision-making by understanding social situation and public opinion.

According to the behavior patterns, daily public relations activities can be divided into:

(1) Constructive activity. In order to open up a new prospect, the organization adopts the method of communication, so as to leave a good impression on the public, and gradually form its own social relationship network.

(2) Maintaining activity. Through various media and with a low profile, public relations practitioners continuously transmit all kinds of information about the organization to the public. Over time, the relevant image of the organization will be perceptible. By accepting the services or products and experience the benefits in person, the public will enhance their favor and recognition of the organization.

(3) Aggressive activity. It means that when the organization conflicts with the public and has serious imbalance with the environment, its survival and development are confronted with resistance and crisis. In order to get rid of the passive situation, the organization takes the offense as the defense, adjusts its relationship with the public, and

tries its best to create a new situation.

(4) Defensive activity. It is a public relations mode in which the organization adjusts its own policies and behaviors to adapt to the public and avoid the imbalance between the two sides when either of them shows signs of friction.

(5) Corrective activity. It is a public relations mode in which the organization takes immediate measures to do remedial work, so as to recover the influence and rebuild the image.

Main Special Activities of Public Relations

Special public relations activities can function in various ways, achieve many goals and bring many benefits to an organization.

(1) They have a single theme closely related to the general goal of public relations, and they can leave a deep impression by adopting a unique activity mode.

(2) They can quickly attract the attention of the public in a relatively short period of time, reach as wide a range of communication as possible, and achieve good public relations effect.

(3) They can give full play to the comprehensive effect of various media and means of communication, form a strong propaganda offensive, and effectively disseminate the organization's information.

▶Press Conference

Press conference is a kind of more formal contact between an organization with the press to maintain a positive relationship. Any social organization, such as the government and enterprises, can hold press conferences. In a press conference held by an organization, the person in charge of the organization or the head of the public relations department generally releases important information about the organization to the press, and then the news will be transmitted to the public through the press. Press conference is one of the best tools for public relations personnel to widely publicize a certain piece of news.

1. Characteristics of Press Conference

First, news release in a press conference, which is formal, grand and high-level, is easy to attract wide attention from the society.

Second, in a press conference, journalists can ask questions according to their interests, which can help better explore the news, fully interview the organization, and at the same time enable the organization to have a deeper understanding of the press. In this form of two-way communication, both depth and breadth of the information are superior to that in other forms.

Third, press conference often takes up more time of journalists and organizers, and more funds are spent, so the cost is higher.

Fourth, press conference has high requirements for the spokesperson and the host. For example, the spokesperson and the host need to be very sensitive and respond to questions quickly.

2. Preparation for Press Conference

First, determine the necessity of holding a reception. According to the characteristics of press conference, it is necessary to analyze and study whether the news to be released is important, whether it has the value of wide dissemination, and also the urgency and best time of the release. Only after confirming the necessity and possibility can a decision be made to hold a press conference. Generally speaking, the factors for social organizations to hold receptions are as follows: (1) emergencies, such as explosions and fires; (2) the proposal of new policies that will have a significant impact on the society; (3) the development of new technologies and products of enterprises; (4) the organization's significant contributions or good deeds to society; (5) the introduction of new measures that will affect the society; (6) the opening, closing, merger and transformation of enterprises; (7) major celebrations of the organization.

Second, determine the scope of the invitees. The scope of the invitees should depend on the scope of the issue or the location of the event. If the incident occurs in a city, the local news reporters are usually invited. The invited journalists should have a larger coverage, including personnel from newspapers, magazines, radio and television, websites and new media.

Third, prepare data. Two aspects of the materials needed for a press conference should be focused: One is the outline of the speaker's speech and report; the other is the relevant auxiliary materials. Relevant staff should get familiar with the theme of the conference in advance so as to prepare the speech draft well. Its content requires an integrated, accurate, and prominent theme. The outline of the speech and report should be circulated within the organization, so as not to cause suspicion among reporters.

The auxiliary materials should focus on the theme of the conference and be comprehensive, detailed, specific and vivid as much as possible. It can include text materials sent to participants, such as pictures, objects and models arranged inside and outside the venue, as well as audio-visual materials to be played during the conference.

Fourth, choose the place and time of the press conference. In the choice of location, the main consideration is to create a variety of convenient conditions for invitees. For example, whether there are auxiliary lights for video recording and shooting, audio-visual aids, slide shows, film playing equipment, etc.; how are the external communication conditions of the venue; whether the transportation is convenient; whether the venue is safe and comfortable without interference; whether the desks and chairs in the venue can facilitate journalists to ask questions and record; etc.

The choice of date should try to avoid holidays and days with major social events, so as not to hamper the reporters from attending the conference.

Fifth, determine the host and spokesperson. Due to the profession and habits of journalists, they often put forward some difficult, profound and even sharp question at the conference, which holds high requirements for the host and spokesperson. The host should be quick in thinking, reaction, and expression, with sufficient cultural consciousness and professional knowledge. The spokesperson of the conference shall be the senior leader of the organization. Because he or she is clear about the overall situation of the organization, including the principles, policies and plans, the answers could be authoritative. If the spokesperson is not competent, necessary training and preparation should be carried out before the meeting.

Sixth, prepare for the journalists' visit. Before the press conference, journalists can be organized to understand the theme of the conference, so as to help them get ready for interview, shoot and video on the spot. Special personnel should be assigned for reception and introducing the settings to be visited.

Seventh, arrange small banquets. In order to maximize the effect of the press conference, small banquets or working meals can be arranged when the organization has sufficient budget. This is also an opportunity to communicate with each other. You can use this occasion to get in touch with the press, collect feedback in a timely manner, and further connect with participants.

In addition, the cost budget should be made ahead the conference according to its size and specification. The cost items generally include site rent, venue layout, printed materials, refreshments, gifts, stationery, audio equipment, postage, telephone, transportation, etc. After sending the invitation letter, telephone confirmation should be made in time.

3. Matters in Press Conference

First, the host and spokesperson should cooperate with each other. The press conference should always focus on the theme set. This requires joint efforts from the spokesperson and the host. For example, when a reporter's question goes too far from the topic, the host should skillfully lead attention back to the topic, and the spokesperson will lead the topic to the theme by answering the question.

Second, for the content that is not to be published or disclosed, we should give an euphemistic explanation to the reporter, who will generally respect the opinion of the host. It can't be simply handled as "I don't know" or "It's a matter of confidentiality".

Third, when encountering a question that cannot be answered, it is not allowed to say "no comment" or "nothing to explain", which will cause dissatisfaction and disgust of the reporters.

Fourth, do not interrupt or stop reporters' speeches and questions.

Even if a reporter has a strong prejudice or makes a provocative speech, the spokesman should not show excitement and gaffe. Standing up and refuting tit for tat is not appropriate.

4. Work after Press Conference

It is necessary to check whether the conference has achieved the expected effect, and the work after the conference mainly includes the following aspects:

First, collect the reports from newspapers and radio stations, then classify and analyze them to check whether the intended goals have been achieved and whether there are mistakes that would cause negative effects. If some problems are found, suitable measures should be put forward to make up for the losses.

Second, check the attendance book of the conference to see if all the reporters present their contributions, and analyze the content and tendency of the manuscripts, so as to serve as a reference for selecting participants in future press conferences.

Third, collect the reaction of reporters and other representatives to the conference, and check whether there is any defect in the whole process, so as to improve the future work.

Fourth, reflect on the relavant conference affairs, draw lessons from them, and file the summary materials for future reference.

▶Opening to the Outside

In order to make the public understand the organization better or to eliminate some misunderstandings, the public relations department is usually responsible for organizing and inviting the public to visit the organization. This kind of public relations activity sometimes has unexpected effects.

The opening of organizations is not only a good public relations activity, but also a series of complicated work. Therefore, it is necessary to carefully study the following issues: (1) purpose; (2) scale; (3) time; (4) personnel; (5) publicity materials preparation; (6) tour route; and (7) reception service.

1. Purpose

Any open visit should have a clear purpose. The public relations personnel should find out what kind of effect can be achieved through the visit, what impression will be left on the audience, and whether there is any material worthy of reporting. With such a clear purpose, a series of activities can be launched around it.

2. Scale

The scale of the visit should be determined beforehand, so as to make corresponding arrangements. If there are only a few visitors, the personnel can accompany them to several departments, introduce the situation, present materials and souvenirs, etc.; if it is a large-scale group visit, it is better to make a comprehensive plan, including the reception time, the number of visitors each time and the opening hours.

3. Time

We should consider not only the time of the open visit, but also the duration required for the whole process. It is better to arrange the opening time on some special days, such as anniversary day, enterprise commencement day, and festivals. Every New Year's Day, Mid Autumn Festival and Spring Festival, Shanghai TV Station invites family members of its staff to visit the station, so that they can be proud and supportive of their relatives working there.

4. Personnel

From the conception of an open visit to the end of the event, senior executives should be involved. To organize large-scale visiting activities, it is better to set up a special committee. The members of the committee should include enterprise leaders, public relations personnel, administrative and human resources department personnel, etc. According to different purposes of the visit, different people should be selected. If the purpose is to introduce and emphasize service or product, the sales department should also be invited.

5. Publicity Materials Preparation

In order to make the open visit a success, the most important thing is to do all kinds of publicity work, including preparing a manual or publicity materials which are simple and easy to understand, and send them to the visitors. A short film, a TV clip or a slide show before the visit can help visitors understand the main profile of the organization. After that, the public relations personnel should guide the visitors to go along the prescribed route and give explanations and answer questions. In order to have a lasting effect, visitors should be presented with a commemorative pamphlet recording the process of the visit and other information about the organization. These pamphlets may be transferred to those who are interested but can't come in person, thus becoming a very useful publicity channel.

6. Tour Route

Plan the tour route in advance to prevent unnecessary troubles and accidents. The leaders of some organizations often worry that the details of some secret technologies or manufacturing process will be leaked due to the open visit. In fact, as long as the arrangement is proper and the guide is skilled, the leakage can be prevented.

7. Reception Service

Visitors should be warmly and considerately received, for example, arrange suitable rest places and prepare sancks and drinks for them. For those who need to entertain and dine, arrangements should also be done in advance; if children are invited, special care should be taken, and toys with organization logos or images will be a good choice.

▶ Exhibition

Exhibition is a form of publicity to show achievements through substances, words, images, charts and so forth.

There are many types of exhibition. (1) In terms of the nature of the exhibition, there are publicity exhibition and trade exhibition. (2) In terms of where the exhibition is held, there are indoor exhibition and open-air exhibition. (3) In terms of the type of goods displayed, there are single commodity exhibition and mixed commodity exhibition. (4) In terms of the exhibition scale, there are large-scale comprehensive exhibition, medium-sized exhibition, small-scale exhibition and pocket exhibition. The most formal and solemn form is exposition.

Exhibitions are welcomed in public relations practice with many advantages: (1) the diversity of media; (2) the intuitiveness of the communication mode; (3) the directness of two-way communication; (4) the efficiency of the communication process.

Much work should be done in holding an exhibition:

(1) Before the exhibition: ① make clear the purpose, theme and type of the exhibition; ② make full preparations for the communication content; ③ send out invitation cards in different ways, and inform the visitors of the theme, type, requirements, time and place of the exhibition; ④ release information to news agencies in an appropriate form; ⑤ prepare for business negotiation; ⑥ the expenses of the exhibition should be carefully estimated and reported to the higher authorities for approval.

(2) During the exhibition: ① the reception work should be arranged and the staff should respect the visitors; ② the press release should be strengthened to collect the feedback from the visitors.

(3) After the exhibition: ① collect and print all kinds of news media reports on the

whole process of the exhibition; ② measure the effect of the exhibition in order to sum up all kinds of experience and find out problems.

▶ Opening Ceremony

Opening ceremony refers to the celebration event held on the first day of large-scale activities such as newly-opened business, exposition, trade fair, completion of important projects or foundation laying.

1. Before the Opening Ceremony

(1) About a week before the ceremony, the guests and journalists should receive the invitation, and the distinguished guests should be confirmed one by one;

(2) Write a warm and solemn speech;

(3) Work out the procedures for the opening ceremony;

(4) Arrange the personnel.

2. General Procedures of Opening Ceremony

(1) Announce the commencement of the ceremony;

(2) Introduce the guests;

(3) Cut the ribbon;

(4) Speeches by relevant leaders and guests;

(5) Other entertainment programs.

3. After the Opening Ceremony

Arrange visitors to discuss with each other, take group photos, etc., and finally do a good job of seeing off the guests.

▶ Sponsorship

Sponsorship refers to the financial and material support provided by enterprises for various public welfare undertakings, and it is a kind of public relations activity in the form of social service.

The role of sponsorship:

(1) Showing that the patrons undertake social responsibility;

(2) Cultivating good impressions on the public;

(3) Advertising some ideas and philosophies.

Types of sponsorship:

(1) Sports activities;

(2) Press and publishing, culture and art undertakings;

(3) Education and scientific research;

(4) Welfare and charities.

Implementation steps of sponsorship:

(1) Determine the person in charge;

(2) Formulate the sponsorship policy;

(3) Conduct preliminary research;

(4) Measure and evaluate the effect.

In May 1990, after receiving a letter for help from Beijing News Agency, Shanghai Dajiang Co., Ltd. decided to independently invest 250,000 yuan in support of *Guangming Daily, Worker's Daily,* sports department of Xinhua News Agency, CCTV sports department, *China Youth Daily, China Sports Daily* and other eight news organizations for the "World Sports Knowledge Grand Prix for the Asian Games". This major event was smoothly launched. During the event, the Organizing Committee of the Grand Prix held a high-level press conference in the Capital Hotel Beijing. Many senior government officials and experts and scholars from the economic circle were invited to summarize the operation and management of Dajiang, which attracted many journalists to Shanghai Dajiang Co., Ltd. and produced "Dajiang series special reports" in major newspapers for several consecutive days. Special reports were also published by CCTV. These publicity reports have made "Dajiang" famous all over the world, producing a strong effect far beyond the investment of 250,000 yuan in advertising and publicity.

►Crisis Management

When an enterprise or organization has a sudden crisis, it should take different countermeasures according to different public objects.

1. Internal Countermeasures

(1) Set up a special agency to deal with the incident promptly. The person in charge of the organization should be the leader of the agency. The public relations department and the personnel of relevant functional departments form an authoritative and efficient working group.

(2) Identify the situation, formulate countermeasures, and request all personnel to unify the caliber and act in coordination.

(3) Reward the excellent performance of staff and summarize the deficiencies.

2. Victim Countermeasures

(1) We should carefully understand the situation of the victims, take responsibility reasonably and apologize sincerely if necessary.

(2) Listen to the victim's opinions calmly, understand and confirm the claims for

compensation.

(3) Avoid arguing with the victim at the scene, even if the victim has a certain responsibility.

(4) Comfort and sympathize with the victims, provide the services they need as much as possible, and do your best to deal with the aftermath.

(5) The compensation methods and standards shall be informed to the victims and their families and implemented as soon as possible.

(6) Certain personnel shall be assigned to contact the victims, and members of the group shall not be changed randomly.

3. Press Countermeasures

(1) It is necessary to unify the caliber of the press and communication circles, pay attention to their wording, and release the information in a way that is most conducive to the organization.

(2) Set up a temporary reception agency for journalists, and assign special personnel to handle the release of news and centralized processing of news coverage related to the event.

(3) On the one hand, we should take the initiative to provide the press with true and accurate information and publicly state the position and attitude of the organization, so as to reduce the speculation of the press and help the press make correct reports.

(4) On the other hand, we must be cautious to spread the news. Before the facts are fully understood, we should not make speculative reports on the causes, losses and other possibilities of the incident, and it's not wise to easily express our support or opposition.

(5) We should show a cooperative, proactive and confident attitude towards the press. Concealment, prevarication and confrontation are unadoptable. For news that is really unsuitable to be published, we should not simply reply with "no comment", but explain the reasons and try to seek sympathy and understanding from the journalists.

(6) Pay attention to reporting from the public's stance and point of view, and constantly provide information of public concern, such as compensation methods and remedial measures.

(7) Apart from news reports, apologies can be published in newspapers and periodicals so as to bear the related responsibilities.

(8) When a report does not conform to the truth, we should, as soon as possible, make a request for correction to the media. Remember to avoid hostility.

In addition to the above-mentioned, appropriate communication countermeasures should be taken for organizations related to the crisis.

We should mobilize all parties to help the organization tide over the crisis as soon as possible, so as to minimize the damage to the organization's image.

Learning to Practice

In October 1993, the National Trade Fair of Washing and Cosmetics was held in Nanjing. Singers, student bands, and public relations personnel gathered at the venue. More than 1,000 enterprises across the country launched a sales promotion war. Huili toothbrush factory from Zhuhai failed to hire public relations staff or a band because it was late. On the morning of the first day, no business was done. Near noon, a reporter from *Jiangsu Business Daily* was photographing the dilemma of the stall. Seeing this, the director of the factory immediately asked him what to do. Suppose you were the reporter, what could you do for the factory director?

Indication for Answer

After thinking a little, the reporter said, "Why don't you do something special and try to hire an old lady to do the PR job?" The director clapped his hands for this novel idea. But who would be most suitable for this role? There was still no ideal candidate for the factory director who had been wandering the streets for more than an hour by taxi. When he arrived at 52 Yunnan Road, the director was attracted by an old lady with strong physique and a good look, so he decided that she was the one he was looking for.

At two o'clock in the afternoon, it was drizzling. When Ms. Xu, the old lady who was dressed in red ribbon and holding up a Huili toothbrush, appeared at the scene, thousands of pairs of eyes were immediately attracted. The result was that 1.8 million pieces of the little toothbrush were sold in one afternoon, and the supply was not adequate to the demand. Nanjing Zhengda Jintai Enterprise Group International Advertising Company tried its best to win the distribution agency right of Huili toothbrush in Jiangsu Province. It is incredible that the factory only spent 50 yuan to carry out this marketing campaign, which was a great success.

On November 28, 1993, Ms. Xu, who had been living at No. 52 Yunnan Road, Nanjing City, received a notice from Zhuhai Huili Toothbrush Supplies Factory to employ her as a product marketing and public relations veteran in Nanjing.

Case Study
PUBLIC RELATIONS

Case 8.1 Pinduoduo Held Press Conference

▶ Replay

On July 26, 2018, Pinduoduo was successfully listed on Nasdaq, and its share price rose nearly 40% on the first day. However, from the second day of listing, news of fake products on Pinduoduo platform appeared on the Internet, including "the 7.5 yuan milk powder", Zheng Yuanjie's reporting about pirated "Pipilu" books, and Skyworth's accusation that Pinduoduo sold counterfeit products.[①]

On July 31, Pinduoduo made several responses. Huang Zheng, founder of the company, released an internal letter, "even if it is a malicious attack, it should be interpreted with good faith". On the afternoon of the same day, Pinduoduo held a press conference at its headquarters in Shanghai. Leaders of the company successively came forward to reply to specific questions from the outside world.

▶ Response

Later, Pinduoduo tried its best to reverse the public's impression about itself by innovation in brand upgrading and supply chain transformation.

On December 12, Pinduoduo announced the launch of the "new brand plan" to provide support for the "foreign famous brand OEM factory" in the "bottom of the food chain manufacturing industry", and decided to carry forward Chinese brands to meet users' need for high-quality products.

▶ Result

According to a research report on e-commerce industry in 2018 released by Aurora Big Data on December 26, Pinduoduo has entered the first camp of e-commerce, accounting for 33.2% of users, second only to 41.8% of Taobao, successfully surpassing Jingdong and Suning.

---

① https://www.sohu.com/a/244468029_100178654?_f=index_betapagehotnews_2.

▶Reflection

In the press conference held by Pinduoduo, inappropriate statements were made, such as "Fake goods are also found on Taobao and Jingdong" "Fake goods are social problems, so it is unfair for 3-year-old Pinduoduo to bear the responsibility". These remarks were seized by the media and spread widely, leaving the public the impression that the enterprise always shirks its responsibilities. But later through the practical improvement, Pinduoduo won support and praise.

Case 8.2 Xiaomi's Activities before New Product Launch

▶Replay of the Event

Xiaomi 9 is a mobile phone released by Xiaomi Corporation at the gymnasium of Beijing University of Technology at 14:00 on February 20, 2019. As a highly cost-effective smart phone, its press conference has always been the focus of the loyal consumers, especially some students and various evaluation bloggers. Before the press conference, Lei Jun, the chairman and CEO, had been disclosing the configuration of the phone from time to time, making it a hot topic all the time. As a result, the first stock was sold out in 53 seconds. This kind of hungry marketing method once again caused a hot discussion among consumers.

Xiaomi 10 is a new type of mobile phone manufactured by Xiaomi Corporation. It is a "high-end flagship mobile phone built for dream" and a masterpiece of Xiaomi's decade. Because of the COVID-19 epidemic, Lei Jun led Xiaomi group to hold an online press conference, which was officially launched on February 13, 2020. This not only impacted the mobile phone industry, but also gave netizens a big surprise.

▶Response

Lei Jun wrote that it was a difficult decision to turn a traditional offline operation into an online one, mainly to cope with the special situation in the epidemic time.

▶Result

The sales volume of Xiaomi 9 was much higher than that of Xiaomi 8. The online launch of Xiaomi 10 set a precedent in the industry. With excellent product quality, Xiaomi 10 has won unprecedented praise. From January to October 2020, the high-end flagship mobile phone series led by Xiaomi 10 sold more than 8 million units worldwide.[①]

▶Reflection

Xiaomi has made good use of the Agenda Setting Theory to effectively influence what facts and opinions people paid attention to and the order in which they talked by providing information and arranging related topics.

At the same time, it has applied the Cultivation Theory, which made the public imperceptibly regard Xiaomi as a representative of China that should be supported.

Case 8.3 There Is Formaldehyde in the Rental Housing of Ziroom

▶Replay of the Event

On August 15, 2018, a WeChat article "Ziroom Is Destroying the City Dream of Young People" was circulated on the Internet. According to the article, by comparing the rentals between Ziroom and other companies' rooms in the same community and the same room type in Hangzhou, it can be concluded that the disguised high interest loan mode of "simple decoration + packing management fee + monthly rent payment" has directly pushed up the rental cost of young people by nearly 20%.

On August 31, WeChat account "Youyouluming" published the article "Ali P7 Employee Died of Leukemia and Rented a Ziroom's Formaldehyde Room before His Death". The article exposed the fact that an Ali employee of P7 level suffered from leukemia after moving in Ziroom's room and died on July 13. The Ali employee had a comprehensive physical examination before moving in, and all physical indicators were normal. His wife came to Hangzhou and tested the formaldehyde in the house, which was showed exceeding the standard.

▶Response

On the afternoon of August 19, Ziroom CEO Xiong Lin issued a statement on rent, industry and Ziroom. The statement said that the price increase in the past six years had been far lower than that of the market as a whole.

On September 1, Ziroom chairman Zuo Hui responded in his WeChat account that "we will accept all criticism, and we will bear all the responsibilities".

---

① http://www.xhsyww.com/2020-11/25/c_139514100.htm.

▶Result

With the passage of time, the heat of Ziroom events gradually decreased. However, it was still being questioned about formaldehyde. On December 6, the case of Beijing tenants jointly suing Ziroom company was heard in People's Court of Dongcheng District, Beijing. A total of 26 Ziroom tenants from Beijing participated in the class action. The reason for the tenants to sue is that they rented a Ziroom house which had just been decorated and painted, and they were not feeling well.

The case of Ali employee's family members suing Ziroom company, which was originally scheduled to be heard in public on September 27, 2018, was granted permission by the court in accordance with the law due to the defendant's application for judicial expertise. Therefore, the specific hearing time was postponed and would be adjusted according to the situation.

At 21:36 on August 3, 2020, netizens complained on tousu.sina.com.cn, Sina's online consumer service platform, that they signed a rental contract on the App a few days ago, and felt dizzy just after moving in for three days. They took out the formaldehyde test paper and found out that the formaldehyde in the house exceeded the standard. At 21:43 on August 3, Ziroom's official account made a reply to the complaints: If the air quality of the room is not up to standard as tested and verified by a professional certification institute, it will conduct unconditional refund and replacement.

▶Reflection

Ziroom's attitude was too arrogant and conceited. For example, on the day before the outbreak of the incident, the leader of Ziroom didn't give a reasonable explanation. But the next day, in his "explanation on Hangzhou tenant incident", he evaded the liabilities with the excuse of waiting for the final ruling.

What should be more criticized is that there were many problems in the implementation of the follow-up treatment scheme. After the formaldehyde storm began, many tenants who applied for air testing were unable to schedule the time. Even after the test, they could not get the report. Most of the test results were orally informed by the housekeeper or customer service, only with the answer that the air was "qualified" or "unqualified", and no specific data could be seen. In addition, reporters found in the investigation that only part of the testing channels were marked with CMA certification testing agency, which was also seriously inconsistent with the company's commitment.

The new-format enterprise, such as Ziroom, doesn't need to hold an open day to help consumers know about the enterprise. The tenants will know the quality of their products and services. It puts forward higher requirements for the operation, especially in the ordinary public relations work.

Courseware   Quiz

Chapter 9

Promotion of Organization Image with Public Relations

Preparation for Start

Scan to Dialogue   Scan to Listen

The employees' view of the organization is a part of the organization's image. You may believe your company is the best business in the tourist industry, and you are even convinced that your company is the leader in this field. I, to tell the truth, am a bit concerned about spending too much time at work. I guess I have to make up for it somehow to speed up my work. But I am ready to accommodate to any task the company asks me to do. These are the actual situations you may encounter at work.

Understanding Objectives

After studying Chapter 9, you should be able to:

1. Define organization image.
2. Analyze an organization's image.
3. Establish an organization image based on CI and CIS.
4. Manage an organization's image.

Basic Concepts and Elements

The core of public relations consciousness is shaping the image of an organization.

Definition of Organization Image

Organization image is the overall feeling, impression and cognition of the organization from both inside and outside views, and it is the comprehensive reflection of the organization's status. The basic characteristics of organization image include: (1) duality of subjectivity and objectivity; (2) duality of dynamism and relative stability.

The image of an organization is the public's opinion or view of the organization, so it is a subjective thing. Because members of the public have differences in social status, values, mode of thinking, cognitive ability, aesthetic standards, life experience and so on, their understanding and evaluation of the same enterprise and its behaviors must be different. In addition, in the process of image building and communication, it is necessary to give full play to the subjective initiative of the organization staff and infiltrate the thoughts, concepts and psychological colors of the enterprise employees.

The material carrier on which the image of an organization depends is objective. The buildings are real, the products are authentic, the employees are concrete, and the activities of the organization are realistic. Therefore, as the reflection of objective things, the organization image is not transferred by human will and cannot be constructed on the basis of illusion.

Organization image is not only from a single person or the minority group, but a collection of the public opinions. Personal opinions are subjective and changeable, but the opinions of the public as a whole are objective.

Types of Organization Image

(1) According to the internal and external performance of the organization, it can be divided into interior image and exterior image.

The interior image of an organization mainly refers to the invisible and intangible parts such as goals, philosophy, spirit and ethos, which is the core part of organization image. The exterior image of an organization refers to the visible and audible parts such as the name, trademark, advertisement, factory building, product appearance and packaging, ceremony and public activities.

(2) According to the subjective and objective attribute, it can be divided into real image and virtual image.

The real image of an organization can also be called objective image, which refers to the actual concept, behavior and material form of the organization. It is an objective existence that is not transferred by human will. The virtual image of an organization is the subjective impression of users, suppliers, partners and internal employees about the whole organization. It is also the impression from the real image through the media and other channels.

(3) According to the scope of recipients, it can be divided into employee's image and outside image.

The employee's image of an organization refers to the overall feeling and cognition of all staff of the organization. The outside image of an organization refers to the cognition formed by the public. On this point, the organization image mainly refers to the outside image.

In addition, according to the evaluation attitude of the public, it can be divided into positive image and negative image. According to the media channels through which the public get the organization's information, it can be divided into direct image and indirect image. According to the public's attention to the factors of the organization image, it can be divided into organization-leading image and organization-auxiliary image.

The organization image consists of the following eight aspects: (1) the product image; (2) the management image; (3) the personnel image; (4) the environmental image; (5) the cultural image; (6) the community image; (7) the logo image; and (8) the media image.

There are usually two kinds of reasons for the damage to an organization image: (1) the misunderstanding of the public, especially the mistakes in the news media reports, or the fictitious rumors; (2) the mistakes made by the organization itself.

Establishment of Organization Image

In order to enhance the consistency and visual impact of organization image publicity, the "CI" (corporate identity) and "CIS" (corporate identity system) strategies should be introduced.

CI originated from the World War I. At that time, the German AEG company took the lead in adopting the trademark designed by de Behans, and applied it to its electrical product series, thus becoming an early representative of the organization and unification of visual image.

CI refers to the symbolic communication system of enterprises to enhance social identity through media, and it is a process of effectively transmitting the business philosophy to the public.

CIS, a corporate identity system, is made up of the mind identity system, the behavior identity system and the visual identity system.

Mind identity system (MIS) is the core and driving force of organizational identity system. It belongs to the consciousness level of ideology and culture. Through MIS, the business philosophy is spread from the inside to the outside. With this intrinsic power, the purpose of recognition can be achieved and the unique organization image can be created.

Behavior identity system (BIS) is a kind of dynamic identity form, which takes the clear and optimized business philosophy as the core, showing the internal system, management, education and other behaviors of the organization, and diffusing the social welfare activities, etc.

Visual identity system (VIS) is a systematic and unified visual symbol system to convey the business philosophy and information of an organization to the outside world. It is the most influential element in the organization identity system. It has the most extensive contact scope and can achieve the purpose of recognition and identification quickly and accurately.

Analysis of Organization Image

The analysis of organization image based on investigation by the organization itself includes the following four aspects: (1) organization reality; (2) staff; (3) management; (4) decision-making.

The analysis of organization image from an outsider includes the following three aspects: (1) public identity; (2) measurement of organization image status; (3) organization image elements.

The measurement of organization image status is mainly carried out in terms of two aspects: popularity and reputation.

Popularity refers to the extent to which an organization is known and understood by the public. It is an objective measure to evaluate the reputation of an organization. It focuses on the evaluation of "quantity", that is, the breadth of the organization's influence on the public.

Reputation refers to the extent to which an organization gains public trust, favor, acceptance and welcome. It is a social indicator to evaluate the reputation of an organization. It focuses on the evaluation of "quality", that is, the depth of the organization's influence on the public.

Four states can be concluded from analysis of the popularity and reputation of an organization:

(1) High popularity / high reputation, indicating that the organization image management is in a good state;

(2) High reputation / low popularity, indicating a relatively stable and safe state of organization image management;

(3) Low popularity / low reputation, indicating that the organization image management is in a bad state;

(4) Low reputation / high popularity, indicating that the organization image management is in a bad state of "infamous".

Organization Image Planning and Management

Every organization hopes to establish a good social image. Therefore, the image should be carefully planned.

The success of organization image planning depends on the coordination and balance between the organizational interests and public interests, the popularity and reputation, as well as the overall image and specific image.

The goal of organization image planning and management is determined by its characteristics which are different from others in three aspects: (1) the unity of subjectivity and objectivity; (2) the unity of commonality and differentiation; and (3) the unity of constancy and flexibility.

The operation procedures of CI planning and management can be divided into three stages.

(1) Organize the field investigation.

(2) Design the CI:

First, transform the abstract concept of recognition into symbolic visual elements;

Second, develop the basic elements to lay a foundation for the overall communication system;

Third, take the basic elements as the basis to develop the image.

(3) Implement the management.

Learning to **P**ractice

Scan to Read More

Dr. Joseph Needham, who specializes in the history of Chinese science, once published an article saying that brandy should be first created in China. Brandy, originally from the Dutch word brandewijn, means "cooked wine". In a narrow sense, it refers to the high alcohol obtained from grape fermentation after distillation, which is then stored in oak barrels. Brandy is often called "the soul of wine". There are many countries producing brandy in the world, and the brandy produced by France is the most famous. For a long time, however, French brandy could not be sold in the United States.

American law once explicitly prohibited the alcohol import. In this regard, although the wine merchants of various countries felt dissatisfied, they were unable to do anything about it.

In 1958, a French brandy company spent a lot of money asking the public in the major newspapers, magazines, radios and television stations in the United States to answer such a question: "The brandy company has two barrels of wine which have been hoarded for 67 years and wants to give them away. Who would be the best receiver?" Soon, the question engulfed the minds of Americans.

Shortly after that, President Eisenhower's 67th birthday was announced by the French in media. It turned out that the two barrels of wine were dedicated to the President to show the respect of the French people. These two barrels of brandy were transported by a special plane. On the President's birthday, a grand ceremony would be held to show the friendship between French and American people. French brandy?! The Americans seemed to think of it all of a sudden. Isn't that a famous wine in the world? Why haven't we thought of tasting it before? At the same time, the history, anecdotes and stories of brandy appeared in various American media.

The long-awaited moment has finally arrived. At ten o'clock in the morning, four handsome French youths, dressed in snow-white palace guard dresses and carrying elegant carriage from the Middle Ages of France, entered the White House square. The barrels carefully designed by French artists were antique and seemed to have given off bursts of mellow wine. When the four young men walked to the White House with the barrels in their hands, the Americans sang *Marseillaise* with thunderous cheers and applause. People were immersed in a happy atmosphere. The major news organizations sent reporters without exception. Reports, pictures and images about the presenting ceremony flooded the major media in the United States on that day.

The distance between brandy and American public has been shortened by the event, which was a very successful public relations activity held by French brandy manufacturers. It directly cleared the way for brandy to enter the American market. Shortly after the presenting ceremony, brandy, which had always been ignored by Americans, quickly became a hot item in the market. Under the background that everyone was proud of drinking French brandy, the wine became a popular product in short supply. And the American authority had to amend the laws to allow the import of brandy out of pressure from the public.

With the popularity of public relations and marketing art, the sales promotion idea of "Wangpo selling melons" (boasting one's goose as swans) is eliminating. There are many praises for French brandy's entry into the American market. What can we learn from this case when we try to improve the sales of product and the image of the organization?

Indication for Answer

Firstly, efforts should be made to shape the friendly image of the organization.

The French factory chosed the President, which was the symbol of the Americans in the World War II, to show its friendship and gratitude. It met the Americans' "savior psychology". While praising the United States, they skillfully displayed and promoted the products, so that the Americans could accept their brandy emotionally.

Secondly, the image of products should be carefully designed.

French artists were invited to design the shape of wine sets and the image of waiters; the wine was transported by a special plane; and the whole process of presenting ceremony was carefully designed.

Finally, we should spread the image of the organization with the help of the media.

Taking the friendship between France and the United States as the starting point and relying on the media to create materials for the news agencies, the publicity activities had high credibility with low costs.

Case Study

Case 9.1 Red Star News Reported Hongmao Medicine Wine

▶Replay of the Event

On December 19, 2017, Tan Qindong, an 39-year-old anesthetist posted a blog entitled "Magical Chinese Tonic Hongmao—a Poison from Heaven". In the article, he questioned the effectiveness of the famous medicinal tonic by analyzing its ingredients and effects. The conclusion, Tan wrote, was that the tonic was not only ineffective, but could actually harm one's health if consumed in excess.

Later, Tan admitted that he used the word "poison" in the hope that it would get the attention of older people, who are more inclined to spend money on such things.[①]

On January 11, 2018, the Public Security Bureau of Liangcheng County, Inner Mongolia Autonomous Region, took Tan Qindong from his home in Guangzhou on suspicion of damaging the company's reputation. Tan Qindong was detained the next day.

▶Response

On April 13, 2018, the Red Star News of *Chengdu Commercial Daily* reported the incident for the first time. After that, some media followed up on the matter. They questioned: "Who gave the power to Hongmao Medicine Wine to capture people across provinces?" On the Weibo and WeChat, many celebrities also put forward similar queries.

After that, in addition to the appropriateness of the trans-provincial arrest, people from all walks of life started to question the false advertising, side effect, over-the-counter drug qualification, and family history of Hongmao Medicine Wine.

▶Result

Tan wasn't the first man to have questioned the pharmaceutical company. In fact, the company has been cited 2,630 times by food and drug authorities in over 25 provinces and cities for false advertising, according to media reports.[②]

However, small fines and punishments from the authorities helped little to stop the company from investing huge amounts of money in advertising. Commercials for the tonic, featuring Chinese film stars and celebrities, can often be seen on Chinese television channels, including CCTV. According to CTR Market Research, the company spent 15 billion yuan ($2.37 billion) on advertising in 2016, and has a revenue of 5 billion yuan annually.

On April 16, 2018, China's Food and Drug Administration Bureau said that over 137 cases of side effect were reported by consumers from 2004 to 2017, and asked Hongmao Pharmaceutical Company to stop its false advertising to the public.

As many people believed, even if the doctor's article has damaged the liquor's image, it should be a civil not a criminal case.[③] The next day, the official Weibo account of Inner

---

① Doctor Tells of Harrowing Arrest after Calling Popular Tonic "Harmful" in Blog[EB/OL]. [2021-8-10]. http://www.globaltimes.cn/content/1099913.shtml.

② Hongmao Medicine Wine's Road of Becoming an Immortal Bao Hongsheng and 2630 Illegal Advertisements [EB/OL]. [2021-8-11]. https://www.thepaper.cn/newsDetail_forward_2029110.

③ Questions to Be Answered in Hongmao Liquor Case[EB/OL]. [2021-8-12]. http://www.chinadaily.com. cn/kindle/2018-04/18/content_36051671.htm.

Mongolia's Procuratorate said it had asked the Public Security Bureau of Liangcheng County to carry out additional investigations and change its coercive measures. Tan was granted bail the same day.

With the gradual decline of people's attention, the whole incident has also gradually ceased. At the beginning of December, 2018, the company was found in the list of "outstanding private enterprises" in Inner Mongolia Autonomous Region, which evoked questions from the media again.

▶Reflection

Hongmao Medicine Wine responded to the doubters in a mighty way and put itself in the spotlight of the media, manifesting its negative reactions and unscientific public relations strategies.

The mistakes caused by an organization itself are generally the main reasons for the damage to its image. Hongmao Medicine Wine should take actions to further eliminate the public's doubts and make progress in its publicity activities.

Case 9.2 Chando Joins Hands with Bilibili to Set up "The Brunch Stream University"

▶Replay of the Event

Since April 2006, Chando, which has established its position in franchise stores and marketing network, has been funding in large-scale advertising. Apart from the annual advertisement in CCTV and local TV stations and a series of integrated marketing activities, it also made use of star endorsement, extensive channel marketing meetings, and systematic marketing training for agents and franchise stores. Chando's marketing strategy is very successful, and has been widely recognized in the industry.

The target group of Chando cosmetica is the young generation—millennials. From October 2019, in order to enter the social circle of young people, Chando has focused on the platform where young people gathered—Bilibili. Bilibili has 15 content divisions, more than 7,000 cultural communities with 110 million active users per month, and more than 1.8 billion interactions per month.

In May 2020, when the video "Houlang" on Bilibili went viral, many brands changed their communication strategies with young people. Instead of blindly catering to and pleasing the new generation, they actively explore the values that meet the spiritual demands of young people, so that they can be convinced of the brand. Together with

Bilibili, Chando released the video of establishing "The Brunch Stream University", advocating a more open attitude to diversified beauty. Many impressive sayings were put forward, "Not everyone has to follow the stream. Just like not all the streams flow to ocean. Be an influencer not a follower." "Don't fear of being different. Chando believes that your uniqueness celebrates your beauty."

▶Response

Chando, together with the uploaders of Bilibili who are representatives of home dance, costumes of Han style, Cosplay, and Lolita, invited young girls with different beauty to voice for the young people's attitude towards life from their respective perspectives.

As well-known uploaders, the girls influence the target audience that the brand hopes to reach in the vertical field. They have more marketing value than KOLs and are the best bridge between the brand and users.

In order to stimulate the enthusiasm for content creation, Chando has also set up "The Brunch Stream University" column on Bilibili, inviting different uploaders to upload all kinds of videos, showing their own circle culture and distinctive beauty, and helping them gain more attention, recognition and exposure.

▶Result

This series of actions helped Chando successfully enter Bilibili, and won the recognition from more young people, and also highlighted the star products of the brand. Users created personalized videos around the products. These creative videos will be transmitted into the brand's own assets and continue to affect the new users later.

▶Reflection

With the trend of younger marketing and the increasing popularity of topics on beauty, Chando is very clever to find the connection point between the target consumers and itself, and chooses to establish "The Brunch Stream University" on Bilibili to accept the diversity and individuality of young girls with a more inclusive and open attitude. On the basis of accurate insight into the psychology of the target group, the co-branded products are carefully developed and designed; Chando makes full use of the platform advantages of the partner, and takes advantage of the opportunity to make the platform its most effective media. Taking advantage of Bilibili, the offline activities of Chando have achieved four key marketing points: entertainment, communication, network and topic. It has successfully achieved face-to-face and accurate communication with young people of all circles, breaking the embarrassment and strangeness of brand communication across the screen. This method not only let consumers intuitively understand the charm of the product, but also established a good image of the brand imperceptibly.

Case 9.3 The Organization Image of BlueFocus

▶ Replay of the Event

On March 15, 2018, an article questioning BlueFocus, the famous public relations company, was spreading on WeChat Moment. The author claimed that he was a former employee of BlueFocus, and was discouraged and threatened to leave by HR department without any compensation. In this article, the author also expressed his suspect that BlueFocus was carrying out a large-scale layoff. It was not surprising that the article has been spreading rapidly and widely, which caused netizens' strong appeal for the truth. On the same day, BlueFocus's stock price slumped.

▶ Response

On the afternoon of March 15, 2008, BlueFocus gave a statement, pointing out that this was only an individual case. This reply didn't show any content of public relations, which was obviously unable to convince the public. Fortunately, BlueFocus did not ignore this incident, and went straight to the root of the crisis, which was within the employees. It first appeased the employees, then communicated with the author in a timely manner, and finally got their understanding and successfully made the author deleted the article and apologized. After solving the root problem, BlueFocus further issued a statement to effectively clarify the matters.

On the evening of March 22, however, author issued another statement: "I deleted the article and made a statement, but got slander and gratuitous dismissal in exchange", which aroused another wave. Soon, BlueFocus refused to show its white feather and issued its second statement. It said the employees should be reprimanded for tearing up the agreement and slandering the company, stressing that a third party team would be set up to investigate the matter.

▶ Result

In June 2018, the Holmes Report, a global authoritative public relations consulting agency, disclosed the 2018 top 10 PR companies around the world and BlueFocus was listed therein for three consecutive years. According to the financial report released on October

28, 2018, the company's revenue in the third quarter was 17.002 billion yuan, a year-on-year increase of 62%; the net profit was 413 million yuan, a year-on-year growth of 48%. Its offshore business increased significantly, while other business sectors grew steadily. Overall, the negative events had little impact on its financial performance.

▶Reflection

In the process of the dismissal incident, both statements of BlueFocus were very timely. Though criticized by many parties for not showing humanistic care or tenderness to its employees, BlueFocue has done a professional public relations job.

Courseware   Quiz

Appendix

Sample Test

Class_____   NO._____   Major_____

►Part I Description of Terms (20 points)

Directions: *Please describe or define the terms of the public relations in English.*

1. Marketing

2. Advertising

3. Research

4. Line functions and staff functions

5. Public relations

►Part II Blank Filling (10 points)

Directions: *Please fill in each blank with a proper word according to the textbook. Pay attention to the forms.*

Public relations in organizations can often be traced back to unintended and humble beginnings. It can begin with someone simply answering letters from customers or members; with someone writing copy for direct mail, 6. _____ advertising, or the annual reports; with someone handling visitors, conducting tours, or arranging the yearly meeting; or with someone serving as an organization's 7. _____ for employees or neighbors. In other organizations, public relations starts as product 8. _____, as news support for a national advertising 9. _____, or as a fund-raising or membership 10. _____.

►Part III Name Questions (20 points)

Directions: *Please spell out the author's name for each of the following famous sayings in the public relations field according to the Effective Public Relations.*

11. The old "flying by the seat of the pants" approach to solving public relations problems is over.

12. The savvy public relations person will have at least a basic understanding of different types of research and the sorts of information the different forms of research can provide.

13. Those who cannot remember the past are doomed to repeat it.

14. All business in a democratic country begins with public permission and exists by public approval.

15. If you issue an untruth in a public statement, it is going to be challenged just as soon as it sees the light.

▶Part IV Essay (50 points)

Directions: *Please write an essay to answer the following questions.*

16. Briefly describe the contributions of the following people to public relations: Ivy Lee, Rex Harlow, George Creel, Edward Bernays, Arthur Page. (10 points)

17. Chester Burger, a long-time consultant in the public relations industry, listed six reasons why an organization retains consulting firms. For example, crucial policy matters require the independent judgment of an outsider. Please list five other reasons why an organization retains consulting firms. (10 points)

18. What do public relations staff expect from line management? (10 points)

19. What do you think about "If you seek stability, then embrace change."? (8 points)

20. What are the four steps of management process of public relations, and what are the main task and question of each step? (12 points)

Keys

References

[1]阿德里安·佩恩等.关系营销[M].北京:中信出版社,2002.

[2]阿尔·里斯,劳拉·里斯.公关第一 广告第二[M].上海:上海人民出版社,2004.

[3]阿克曼.形象决定命运[M].北京:中信出版社,2002.

[4]安岗.安岗公共关系论谈[M].北京:人民日报出版社,1992.

[5]陈先红.现代公共关系学[M].北京:高等教育出版社,2017.

[6]达文波特·贝克.注意力管理[M].北京:中信出版社,2001.

[7]戴维斯.大众传播理论[M].北京:清华大学出版社,2013.

[8]迪尔特丽·布雷肯里奇.新公共关系手册:成功的传媒关系策略[M].北京:中国人民大学出版社,2003.

[9]弗雷泽·西泰尔.公共关系实务[M].北京:清华大学出版社,2017.

[10]格伦·布鲁姆.公共关系[M].北京:中国人民大学出版社,2013.

[11]何春晖.中外公关案例宝典[M].杭州:浙江大学出版社,2011.

[12]胡百精.公共关系学[M].北京:中国人民出版社,2018.

[13]居延安.公共关系学[M].上海:复旦大学出版社,2008.

[14]卡特利普等.公共关系教程[M].北京:华夏出版社,1998.

[15]肯特·沃泰姆.形象经济[M].北京:中国纺织出版社,2004.

[16]李智允.全英义面试攻略大全[M].上海:上海社会科学院出版社,2017.

[17]伦纳德·萨非尔.强势公关[M].北京:机械工业出版社,2002.

[18]马克·麦希斯.媒体公关法则[M].广州:广东经济出版社,2004.

[19]迈克尔·里杰斯特.危机公关[M].上海:复旦大学出版社,1995.

[20]桑德拉·奥利佛.战略公关[M].北京:科学普及出版社,2004.

[21]威尔伯·施拉姆等.传播学概论[M].北京:北京大学出版社,2007.

[22]殷娟娟.公共关系学教程[M].北京:中国人民大学出版社,2017.

Postscript

I remember that there was a period of time in the 1980s, when large-scale meetings, lectures and lecturer groups seemed to be very popular. When I read those speeches, I didn't know why there were so many people clapping at that time. I have read a book on giving lectures many times, because I always want to find the secret of charming all the audience. I used to read a magazine called *Speech and Eloquence* and took a lot of notes by hand. I have also read some books in Mandarin trainning.

After entering the university, I finally saw various shows on the spot. However, I forgot about the shows, and was impressed by the way the host talked. A teacher of mine said that it was all about public relations personnel's practicing bravery. Therefore, when I heard that they were going to organize a Public Relations course, I quickly signed up. One of the training classes was given by our modern Chinese teacher, Mr. Zhou, who was equivalent to a "male god" in the current time. Nowadays as soon as I find out the training certificate, I can see the figure of Mr. Zhou in my mind, who later became the Vice Principal.

In 2002, I was preparing to go to Suzhou University to study for a doctorate. The school hasn't started yet in August, when I received a phone call from my teacher, whose wife asked me to take a part-time job in public relations at Wenzheng College of Suzhou University. I went to Suzhou ahead of time and lived in the dormitory of my senior brother. One evening, I was nibbling on the textbook by Ju Yan'an, a professor of Fudan University, and happened to encounter a Public Relations class set by the School of Management. I was quite sure that I could go to this class once a week. There were shuttle buses and free lunch every time. But after two rounds, I gave up the class because I had to write a paper. And my major is Comparative Literature and World Literature, not Management or Journalism. From Hengyang Normal University to Shaoxing University, the courses I taught were basically in the field of literature and art, and the title of mine was also in Chinese.

After I transferred to Zhejiang Yuexiu University in 2014, I began to teach Chinese. Later, I started to teach a bilingual course in Public Relations. In 2017, I applied for a key project in Shaoxing, and presided over the compilation of teaching materials. In 2018, the course became a bilingual demonstration model of the school. In 2019, the teaching materials were approved as a Zhejiang Province 13th-Five-Year Plan New Type Teaching Material Project.

The bilingual course of Public Relations has been taught for eight rounds, but I think the knowledge points of the textbook can't be finished in one class. In the summer of 2020, I reconstructed the teaching materials into a textbook, which focuses on the main principles of public relations. In each chapter, there are two or three cases, all of which occurred from 2017 to 2020. At the very beginning of each chapter, warm-up exercises which are called Preparation for Start are provided to stimulate students' interest in learning public relations knowledge. What goes after that is Learning to Practice and Indication for Answer to inspire students to think and solve real public relations problems with the knowledge they have learned.

Many thanks shall go to the leaders of the Institute of Network Communication, who have always attached great importance to the publication of this textbook, and the editors of Zhejiang University Press have also paid a lot of efforts. However, due to the lack of time, there are inevitably some shortcomings in this book. Readers, especially experts and my college peers, please don't hesitate to contact and inform me if any mistake is found.